CHINESE FOREIGN DIRECT INVESTMENT IN AFRICA

Mauro Santos

Lulu Publishing Services rev. date: 10/08/2019

Contents

Figures Index

Table Index

Dedication

I would like to dedicate this work to all those who have helped me and allowed for the preparation and completion of this project.

Also, I dedicate this work to my family, my closest friends, my tutor, and other faculty members who have encouraged me to complete this first phase.

Thank You Note

To my teacher and adviser, Dr. Paulo Reis Mourão, who with his great expertise and vast knowledge, encouraged and motivated me to carry out this thesis. It was a project that required many hours of research and econometric work and was only possible thanks to his great dedication.

To a few close friends who also helped and encouraged me, and to my family who helped me greatly throughout the whole process.

In particular, I thank and dedicate this project to my parents who have supported me in every way imaginable, allowing me to follow this work to the end, without their indispensable support, none of this would have been possible.

Introduction

The basis of this project was founded in wanting to research the causes for Chinese investment in Africa, by analysing 48 African countries in particular.

Over the past few years we have seen a major Asian expansion, notably involving the main FDI source countries: China and India. However, this study only involved one of these FDI source countries, China.

During the last period of crisis, which started during 2008, the Chinese economic model developed, together with all of its investments, both domestically and internationally. It was also noted that not only the Chinese, but also international investors turned their attentions towards Africa.

This theme is interesting, not only from a stand point of international politics, but also of the international economy, having been studied by many authors, often focusing on subject at an international level. Many hypotheses have been drafted relating to Chinese interest in Africa, covering such subject as economic, strategic, political, military and even demographic interests.

Several authors (detailed in this work) try to uncover the reasons for Chinese investment in Africa, suggesting several theories such as the need for natural resources, namely coal, iron ore and the ever vital "black gold" – oil; others site vast and numerous African market. Other authors refer to the need to obtain agricultural products in order to secure food sources for the Chinese population.

This work consists of four main chapters. The first is an introduction that presents the main theme. The second, a brief summary of the literature reviewed relating to the topic in question, presents relevant concepts and ideas to be used in order to address questions, as well as addressing the selection of variables used for the study. The third covers the development and treatment of information collected, as well as presenting the model studied and results obtained. Finally, the fourth and final chapter is a short summary of the work, focusing on results collected and their meaning.

For this study was used the GMM econometric model in order to evaluate over 48 African countries between the years of 2003 and 2008. The complete database and other relevant information can be found in the appendix.

1

Determinants for Foreign Direct Investment (FDI) - A literature review

1.1. Notion and evolution

1.1.1. Notion

In order to start this thesis, it is first necessary to define Foreign Direct Investment. Foreign Direct Investment (FDI) is adopted by companies in order to encourage internationalisation. However, FDI is not only an opportunities generator; it also entails risk, related not only to the economic environment, but also to social and increasingly political environments.

Foreign Direct Investment is defined as a component of national financial income[1]; it is foreign investment in domestic structures, equipment and organisations, excluding direct investment in stock markets.

This type of investment is considered more useful than investment through multinational companies, as the latter is considered *hotmoney* and can *evaporate* at the first sign of any local destabilisation; the same is not true of FDI, according to McQueen authors (2004).

---

[1] FDI is a component of the financial balance of a country, and is inserted into capital and financial accounts, according to Sachs and Larrain (2000).

FDI's are also long-term initiatives taken by an investor broker of country 'A' involving country 'B'. Joint venture, as defined by a form of alliance between two or more legally independent entities is usually involved in order to share business, investment and profit risk associated with a particular project.

Historically, joint ventures have been established between non-competing companies (or other organisations), generally in order to ensure the completion of the different implementation processes. However, this type of relationship is increasingly being observed between competitors, especially concerning projects related to technological development, due mainly to the large cash volumes required during the implementation phase. Special attention is given to joint ventures established between companies wishing to expand into international markets; in this case, the companies both hold investments abroad, dividing among themselves the business risks. We can thus carry this concept to a project interstate relationship, and so correlate Chinese FDI policies with projects in African countries. This is possible as most Chinese credit lines and funds are directed directly into projects.

There are two types of FDI:

- Inward FDI (when country A receives country B's FDI); and
- Outward FDI (when country B sends FDI to country A).

Capital from inward FDI tends to be invested into local resources.

Outward FDI is also referred to as investment abroad, in this case it is local capital being invested into a foreign resource. This can also be found in the form of import and export agreements between a foreign country. This type of FDI is very successful in conjunction with a risk coverage guarantee implemented by the government.

According to the OECD definition, FDI reflects the objective of obtaining lasting interest by a resident entity in economy A. Economy B contains a resident entity that does not belong to the investor.

In accordance with the OECD, it is recommended that a Direct Investment Company should be defined as such when it holds 10% or more of a company's ordinary shares or local voting power.

This 10% determines the existence of a direct investment relationship. The holding of at least 10% implies that the investor is able to influence or participate in company management, thus not requiring absolute control of the investment in order to influence decisions.

There are countries that consider that a direct investment relationship is present when a combination of the following factors can be observed:

- *Representation in the boards of directors;*
- Participation in the decision-making process;
- Intercompany material transactions;
- Interchange of managerial personnel;
- Provision of technical information;
- Provision of long-term loans at lower rates than those existing on the market.

1.1.2. Evolution of Foreign Direct Investment - A Global Perspective

We will now continue with a short summary describing the historical evolution of Foreign Direct Investment.

During the years that followed the Second World War, Foreign Direct Investment (FDI) was dominated by the United States of America, the dominant global power at the time and one of the significant beneficiaries of this conflict that devastated much of Europe.

Between 1945 and 1960, the US accounted for three-quarters (75%) of global FDI, due mainly to the investment made by the US into Europe, according to the site www.fdi.net.

Following on from this period, FDI became a worldwide phenomenon and has since been growing continuously, presently accounting for more than 20% of overall global GDP. This is due largely to the diverse forms that FDI has taken on over the past years, that is, while FDI was principally seen as a means for some countries to have access to specific products or materials, as well as being a unilateral investment, it developed as a result of increasing globalisation, becoming more multilateral and diverse. This phenomenon is now so widespread that some emerging countries are already major FDI recipients, as well as large investors in developed economies, as is the case of China and India, which are preferred places in terms of investing FDI but who also invest in all parts of the world.

The FDI became bilateral in many cases, i.e. Country X invests into a particular sector in country Y and country Y invests into another sector of Country X.

It is becoming increasingly difficult to distinguish between FDI investor and recipient countries has there is increasing financial interconnection between countries in general. We observe cases involving African countries such as Angola, who are major recipients of Chinese FDI, but who are at the same time investing in such countries as Portugal, just as China receives large investments from European countries, and reinvests into several European economies and on a large-scale into the US economy.

FDI models are varied and have evolved over the years, differing from country to country and sector to sector, i.e. there is no fixed or pre-defined template for FDI.

FDI evolution is the product of the evolution of international economic relations over the past decades, and is driven by all kinds of economic, social and scientific advances.

However, as Figure 1 shows (see graph on next page), the real revolution of FDI occurred over the past two decades, due largely not only to the growth of BRIC (Brazil, Russia, India, China), which are major investors worldwide, but also to the development of several African economic powers which possess vast and promising markets at all levels, from raw material supplier markets to internal consumer markets.

Figure 1 - FDI flows, global and by economic groups,
1980-2009 (amounts in billion USD)

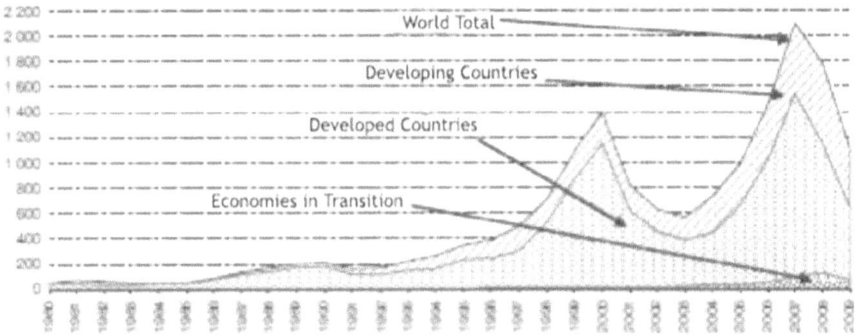

From the data shown in Figure 1 (see picture above),we can make a brief analysis of the evolution of Foreign Direct Investment.

This analysis will give more emphasis to the last two decades. As is clearly observed, the1980'swere almost entirely dominated by FDI between developed countries.

However, it is observed that, since 1987, FDI entering developing countries has been growing continuously up until the present day, following global economic growth and contraction trends.

Using figures presented by the World Investment Report of 2010, it was possible to formulate the following Tables:

Table 1 - FDI Stock (Inward), by region, 1990/2000/2009

Year	World (10^6dollars)	Developed economies (10^6dollars)	% of total	Developing economies (10^6dollars)	% of total
1990	2,081,782	1,557,248	74.80361	524.526	25.19601
2000	7,442,548	5,653,182	75.95762	1,728,455	23.22397
2009	17,743,408	12,352,514	69.61748	4,893,490	27.5792

Source: WorldInvestmentReport 2010

5

Table 1 shows, that despite an increase in the percentage of FDI stocks in developing countries, over these three periods, this increase is declining.

Table 2 - Flows FDI (Inward), by region, 2007-2009

Year	World (10^6dollars)	Developed economies (10^6dollars)	% of total	Developing economies (10^6dollars)	% of total
2007	2,099,973	1,444,075	68.76636	564.930	26.90177
2008	1,770,873	1,018,273	57.50119	630.013	35.57641
2009	1,114,189	565.892	50.78959	478.349	42.93248

Source: WorldInvestmentReport 2010

Table 2 shows that between 2007 and 2009, the amount of FDI moving from developed to developing countries has increased. The trend is significant as it shows that, over a period of just three years, the percentage of FDI directed to developing economies rises from 26% in 2007 to around 43% in 2009. This trend is also shown in Figure 2, whereby a growing equilibrium between developed and developing countries, towards the year of 2009, can be observed.

However, these figures depict global values, and so it is necessary to break down these values and analyse those relating to African countries in general.

These African countries have been the centre of media attention for many years due to a large concentration of global FDI over the past decades which have originated from many diverse sources, including China.

Figure 2 - FDI flows (%)

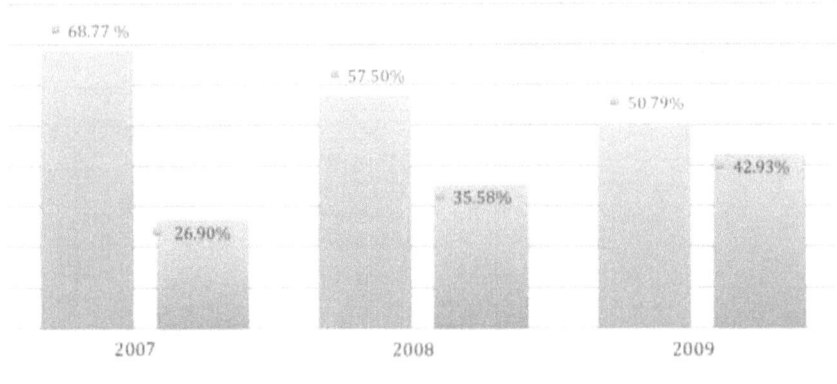

Source: WorldInvestmentReport 2010

According to Cho (2003), globalisation is inevitable, irreversible and is the most important process of the millennium dealing with the capitalisation of globalisation by emphasising positive and mitigating negative aspects. Globalisation has increased opportunities for success, but has also exposed developing countries to new risks.

So, in this context, Globalisation is understood more as an economic and financial concept and can be defined as an opening and / or deepening of links of national economies to a 'global market' of goods, services and especially capital.

FDI has been one of the key elements of globalisation and the world economy over the last two decades and has grown at an unprecedented rate, with a brief interruption during the recession of the early 1990s, as shown by the following chart:

Figure 3 - FDI flows, 1999-2010

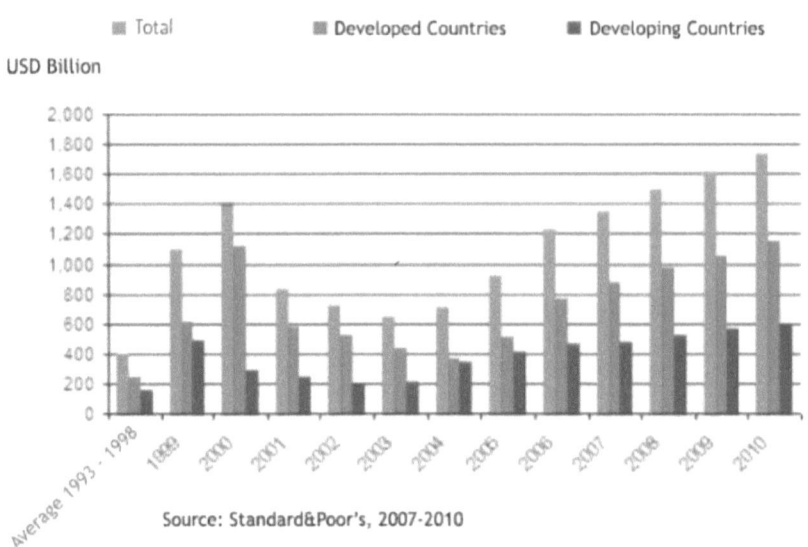

Source: Standard&Poor's, 2007-2010

The last decade has seen an unparalleled opening and modernisation of economies in all regions of the world involving monopolisation, privatisation, participation of private provisioning infrastructures and simplification of tariffs.

1.1.3. Evolution of Chinese Outward FDI

According to Davies (2009), in 2008 global FDI fell by about 20%, while Chinese FDI almost doubled. This disparity is likely to continue in 2009 and 2010, as China increasingly invests abroad.

Chinese FDI began in 2000 as the result of the adoption and promotion of a GO GLOBAL policy designed to stabilise local champion companies and international stake holders. From an annual average of USD 453 million (US dollars) in 1982-1989 and 2.3 billion between1990-1999, this amount of FDI rose to USD 5.5 billion in 2004, USD 12.3 billion in 2005, USD 17.6 billion in 2006 and USD 24.8 billion in 2007.

According to the data released by the Chinese Ministry of Commerce (February 2009) the cumulative FDI value stood at USD 118 billion in 2007 and was predominantly in the tertiary sector, representing about 70% of the total, the secondary sector representing about 16% with the remaining 14% being channelled into mining and oil production.

One of the most prevalent reasons shown by the international averages and in some academic work is the need for China to secure natural resources in order to fuel rapid growth, yet this is not the area of greatest significance relating the Chinese investment.

Government support, including Official Development Assistance (ODA), has been crucial to this investment with regards to leveraging resources. The largest Chinese companies have also come to acquire several global brands such as IBM and Rover. Large state-owned enterprises in China are diversifying internationally and thus losing their local monopoly.

Some companies, despite having access to a large, local labour force, are choosing to relocate labour-intensive departments abroad to areas such as Vietnam and African countries where labour is cheaper.

Chinese investment has not experienced proportional growth in all parts of the world and did not occur simultaneously but rather, an allocation of values by regions occurred around the globe at different time periods. These investments have harboured and continue to show a supported investment logic, both relating to the Chinese market or local political interests and always following global trends.

During the early 90s the "bulk" of Chinese outward FDI was directed towards North America. However, recently we have witnessed a change in that most outward FDI is now been sent to Asian countries. During these transitional periods, there were periods when large sums of investment were allocated to Latin America, but in recent years China has turned its attention to investment in Africa due to a number of factors covered by the following paragraphs.

According to a UNCTAD press release during 2007, there has been a steady growth of FDI directed towards Africa from Asian countries, much of it turned towards natural resources. UNCTAD then went on to state that with the implementation of the right policies, it could be possible to channel this FDI towards other sectors such as industry. During the past few years, China has become one of the biggest investors and trading partners of Africa.

According to a magazine article from *Exame Angola*, "The World in 2011", China would experience growth of 9.6% and in Africa there are countries with growth rates of around 7% or more. A study carried out by the IMF (International Monetary Fund), referring to this same article, concludes that while developed countries have growth rates of 2%, emerging countries and developing countries have rates of around 6.4%.

According to the same source (*Exame Angola*) it is possible to conclude that the 'crown jewels' of global economic growth will be China, India, Brazil and some countries / regions in Africa.

Figure 4 - Help by year and region, 2003-2007

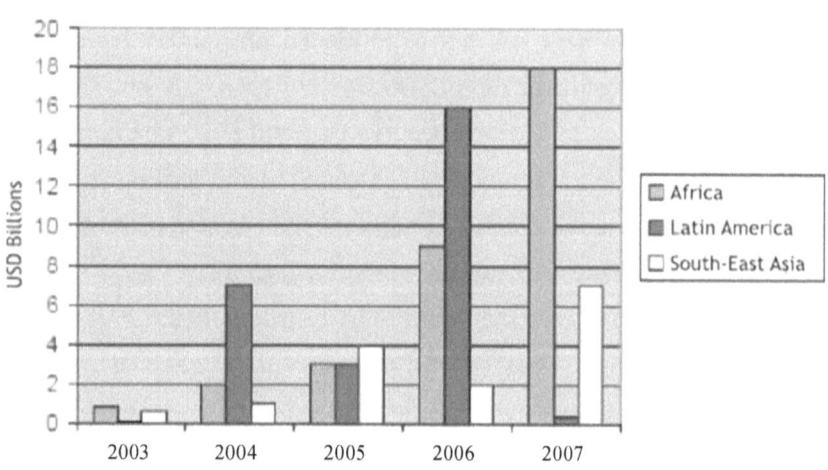

Source: WorldInvestmentReport 2010

As Figure 4 (see image above) shows, we can see a rapid change in USD amounts provided as Official Development Assistance and correspondingly in Chinese investment, moving from Latin America to Africa.

1.1.4. Trade relations between China and Africa

"The Chinese offer us concrete and the West intangible values such as transparency, good governance... what good is all of this if people do not have access to electricity or employment? Democracy is not something you eat[2]."[2]Serge Mombouli, counsellor of the Congo Presidency quoted from *The Chinese Safari.*

Taking this *leitmotiv* of Mombouli into account, we can move on to the discussion of trade relations between China and Africa, whereby we can see that with the opening of the FDI market at a global level, together with the continued growth of the Chinese financial market, that there was an incentive for Chinese investment in Africa.

Part of the investment begins with base support sectors such as roads or dams, the joining of small neighbourhood areas, or in some cases, the construction of entire cities. Another part of this investment passes through the primary sector, i.e. the agricultural or extractive sector. We note that there is growing Chinese interest in African land purchase, fuelled by a constant need for food resources. Investment into the extractive sector, contrary to what has been said, is not unique to the oil sector or to energy resources such as natural gas and coal, but also covers the mining and forestry extraction sectors. Another important sector is the Public Works sector, where we observe large amounts of Chinese investment, either as a single entity or as part of an interstate cooperation. These investments are made with several counterparts and are normally less stringent than

---

[2] Michel, S. and M. Beuret, 2009, The Chinese Safari, Don Quixote Publications, P. 11.

those imposed by other countries or international organisations. Many of these payments are of economic nature, that is, they pass through a series of government concessions. These concessions are preferred by countries with resources that do not have the means to explore in the short-term capacity or enforce the rules or terms imposed by developed countries.

The services sector is a major destination of mostly private Chinese investment that supplies the much in need, large African market with low cost goods.

In order to support what has been written previously, we analysed the following tables which show the goods and assets utilised during Sino-African trade.

Table 3 –A Summary of Africa's exports to China.

Main products exported from Africa to China	Major exporting countries
Crude	Angola, Sudan, Congo, Guinea
Wood	Congo, Guinea
Iron and concentrates	South Africa, Mozambique
Ores and concentrates of non-ferrous ores	South Africa, Congo, DR Congo, Nigeria
Diamonds	South Africa
Cotton	Congo
Tobacco	Zimbabwe
Iron and steel coils	South Africa
Platinum	South Africa
Concentrated manganese ore	Gabon, South Africa
Copper and copper alloys	Zambia, South Africa, Congo
Aluminium	South Africa
Non-coniferous species of wood	Gabon, South Africa, Congo

Source: Broadman and Isik (2007)

Table 4 –A Summary of China's exports to Africa

Main products exported from China to Africa	Major importing countries
Clothes and textiles	South Africa, Ethiopia, Sudan, Nigeria
Shoes	South Africa, Nigeria
Motorbikes	Nigeria, Guinea
Batteries	Nigeria

Rice	Nigeria
Bags, pursues	South Africa, Nigeria
Constructions Material	Nigeria, South Africa, Angola, Sudan

Source: Broadman and Isik (2007)

Figure 5 - Trade between China and Africa, 2007

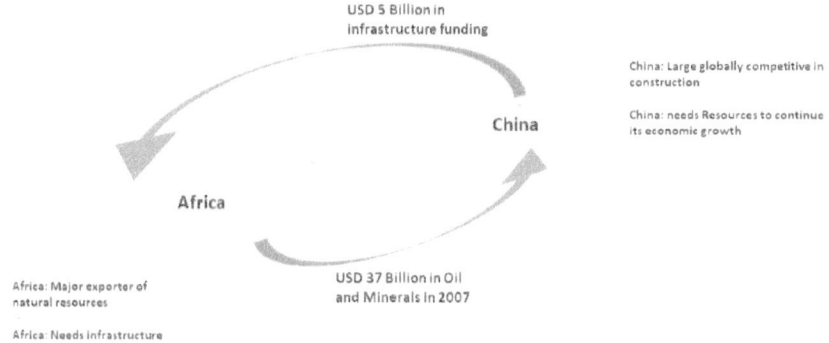

Source: WorldInvestmentReport 2010

By also analysing Figure 5, we can conclude that China has been a key economic partner for Africa.

Figure 6 - Trade between China and Africa, 1995-2005

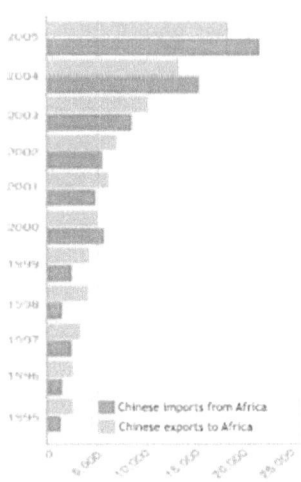

Source: WorldInvestmentReport 2010

Figure 6 shows trade between China and Africa in 2007. We can see that there was an increase of bilateral trade between the two countries between 1995 and 2005.

1.1.5. Evolution of Inward FDI in Africa

It is fairly usual these days to read articles in newspapers or magazines covering the large investments that are made in Africa. Although not an entirely new subject, it is nevertheless a matter of present day interest. The reality is that every day huge sums are being invested into Africa in several areas, covering all sectors (primary, secondary and tertiary), and that these sums are constantly increasing in value. Africa is no longer just a commodity market, but also a consumer and financial market; we come to this conclusion by taking into account both the historical development and natural conditions of the continent together with the growing need for resources and markets which leads to a natural expansion of the financial market.

The previous paragraph is illustrated in Figure 7.

Figure 7 - Chinese FDI flows to Africa

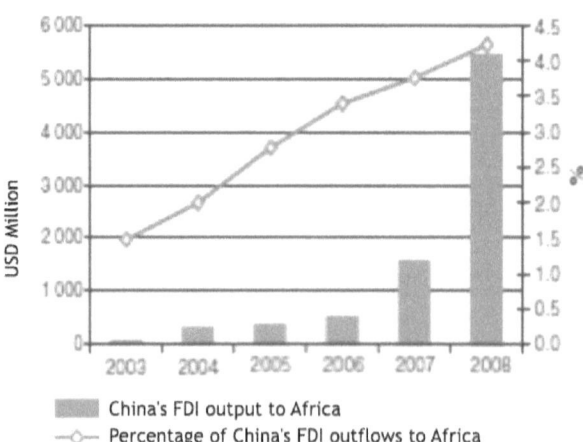

■ China's FDI output to Africa
—◇— Percentage of China's FDI outflows to Africa

Analysing these graphs, we can observe the evolution of the commercial relations of one of the biggest world markets with the African market. Also, we can conclude as to why this continent is growing at the same rate as global market leaders. According to the Angolan newspaper, Jornal de Angola, 03.16.2010, which draws upon a conclusion sited by the President, the African continent has been resilient against the crisis.

One of the factors that has contributed to this increase is the growing political stability on the continent which is directly reflected in the economy, and as we say, common sense, 'investment generates investment'.

Another major contributing factor to this increase is the importance of this market in relation to investment coming from new emerging countries, for example the BRIC. This activity also leads to an increase in investment from other countries that are trying to monitor the market for several reasons.

So, it is natural for large amounts of FDI to be directed towards a continent where returns are faster, and security is ever improving.

There are several infrastructure short falls which leads to easier investment opportunities from an innovative or technological point of view and also massive potential for generating large growth rates at all levels, namely economic, social and political.

We must now analyse the importance of this FDI in relation to Africa itself, that is, what advantages does this FDI bring to African countries

1.1.6. Why is FDI considered important to Africa?

"... The influx of Chinese shops was met with a mixture of enthusiasm and concern, reflecting the ambivalent impact it has on the local economy" (Alden, 2009).

The latest economic report on Africa drafted by the United Nations Economic Commission for Africa advocates that FDI is the key to solving economic problems.

Other entities, such as the IMF and the World Bank, suggest that large FDI flows will result in economic development. Governments in sub-Saharan Africa are eager to attract this type of investment. These investments are no longer only job and *spillover* creating mechanisms for the economy, but also promote competitiveness which helps addressing the lack of economic resources.

African countries are inclined to attract FDI. Their reasons differ, but can be summarised as follows:

- Lack of capital resources;
- Intensification of internationalisation;
- Need for efficient management techniques;
- Technological needs;
- Job creation opportunity.

These reasons are seen as means of developing the local economy either through job creation, which in fact does not always happen, or as a result of the implementation of new technology via *spillover* that will transfer to the local economy and economic agents.

However, job creation is not always what you expect because everything depends on the type of FDI that will arise. Many studies indicate that generally, in these developing countries, the jobs created are of low income and do not lead to higher living standards.

According to Alden (2009), there are several political policies that are implemented in order to attract FDI, including:

- Tax incentives;
- Financial incentives;
- Incentives relating to the alteration of applicable rules.

Also, according to Alden (2009), there are other factors that directly influence FDI, the most important being:

- Privatisation programmes;
- Economic determinants such as market size and per capita income;
- Economic determinants of FDI related to natural resources;
- Economic determinants related to efficiency, production costs of intermediate goods, infrastructure;
- Political and social stability, and rules and agreements relating to FDI.

1.1.7. Chinese investment model in Africa: 'favour-able loans from the Chinese government and Preferential Credit to the Buyer / Exportation"

In this chapter we will not describe contracts and credit in detail, but will outline its contours and lines in a more general form.

We can observe a kind of political and economic relationship model between China and African countries. This model is known as the "Angola model". This model shows a growing trend which involves China making loans through the Eximbank, the only line of credit within these contracts. As a rule of thumb, these loans are called upon based on an investment project into social or industrial infrastructure.

These credit concessions are a foreign policy tool, especially in African countries that lack monetary resources, that have great potential in natural resources and especially those that are in deficit with poor network infrastructure. These financial arrangements are also important as they maintain a lower level of Chinese unemployment tax rates, as can be observed with Chinese companies that have the right to receive the contract; this is one of the mandatory conditions for contracts with the Eximbank. These contracts tend to be long-term and involve interest rates well below those assigned by the financial markets or other countries. The loan receiving countries ensure that the interest is secured by the contractual obligation to provide a particular product or natural resource for a certain time period, or at a certain price.

It is often assumed that Chinese companies are less aware of the risks of investing in Africa, but this is not true; the reality is that Chinese banks bear the costs and facilitate interest that guarantees the security of Chinese companies by connecting them to the State. These counterparts act as guarantors for the resources that the major economic power that is China so badly needs.

This credit works like a current account held in China on behalf of the debtor country and provides direct payment services to Chinese companies, thus ensuring that the capital remains within the Chinese domestic economy.

This Chinese approach to Africa refers to a "coalition of investments" between various sectors, i.e., these investments are made in areas that complement each other and between economies that are complementary in terms of needs. It is worth noting that there are highly visible cases whereby the Chinese invest both in construction and in the extraction of natural resources, as in the following examples of Angola, Gabon and Zimbabwe.

ANGOLA

The contract for a loan of USD 4.5 billion granted for the reconstruction of infrastructure in exchange for the negotiated conditions of a LIBOR rate of interest plus 1.5% in percentage points over 17 years, including a grace period of five years. Thus, China ensures the supply of 10 thousand barrels of oil per day, at the market price of the day and a minimum of 50% of services, materials, technologies and equipment must originate from China.

ZIMBABWE

In the case of Zimbabwe, China provides 58 billion for agricultural equipment in return for tobacco supply.

GABON

In the case of Gabon, a contract was signed giving China sole exploration rights to iron rich deposits located in Belingo, with an initial investment of 590 million.

Figure 8 - "Angola Model"

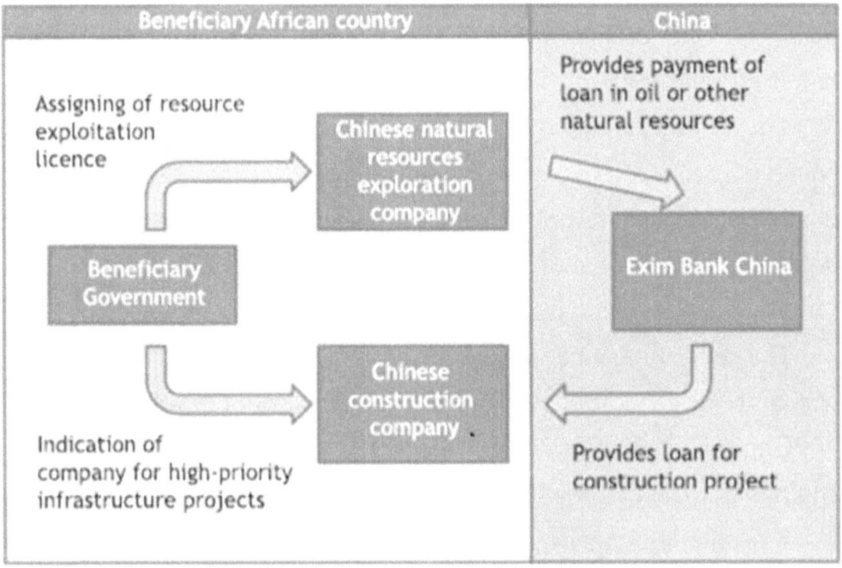

Source: Sebastian (2008)

The following paragraphs will cover the contract itself, or rather the general outlines of the agreement, taken from the Eximbank of China:

The basic concept associated with these favourable loans from the Chinese Government covers medium or long-term loans at reduced interest rates, made by Eximbank, that are authorised by the Chinese government for official assistance purposes.

Objectives of favourable loans:

- Finance industrial projects, construction of infrastructure and social welfare projects in the country asking for credit, which can generate economic returns and benefits for society;
- Finance the country requesting the loan enabling the purchase of Chinese technology, including electrical and mechanical products or services and other goods.

At first, the loan amount should not be less than 20 million RMB (20 RMB = 3.04554 US dollars, exchange rate as of March 2011).

Interest and maturity rates will be discussed between the governments of both countries (Chinese Government and the Government requesting the loan).

The criteria of the projects have to meet certain conditions and must be approved by the two governments. The Government that asked for the loan must have stable diplomatic relations with China and must be politically and economically stable. It should be a country with the ability to pay credit, and have a history of contractual compliance.

The project must be viable and must involve vital sectors that contribute to the economic growth and social benefit of the country.

Chinese companies will be selected as the project contractors. The equipment must be provided principally by a Chinese exporter.

Also the equipment, materials and technologies must at least be of 50% Chinese origin and additional project funds must be readily available.

1.2. FDI determinants

1.2.1. The impact of political risk on Foreign Direct Investment

According to Aguiar and Gulamhussen (2009), Foreign Direct Investment (FDI) is implemented by companies in order to internationalise. FDI creates both risks and opportunities; these relate not only to economic but also to social and, increasingly, political growth. Incidentally, Aguiar and Gulamhussen (2009) show how the control of corruption, host country government efficiency and political stability of the host market can boost FDI inflows. Also relating to this subject, Acemoglu (2001) discusses regulatory quality as correlated with attracting FDI.

Many studies have been carried out in order to determine the factors that lead developed countries to invest in developing or emerging countries with (not infrequently) unstable economies (Bellak et al., 2008). One factor that could traditionally discourage FDI implementation was high inflation rates that a country (potentially the receptor) will manifest (Bellak et al., 2008).

According to the OECD, this is a kind of international investment made by a resident entity in one country (direct investor) with the objective of establishing a lasting interest in a resident enterprise in a country other than that where the investor is registered (direct investment enterprise). "Lasting interest" implies the existence of a long-term relationship between the direct investor and the enterprise, with a significant degree of influence exerted by the direct investor on the management of the receiving company.

FDI involves the transfer of a set of resources to a foreign market, including access financial capital, technology, know-how, management skills, leadership.

In the next subchapter, I will outline the policies that countries generally tend to follow with regards to attracting FDI. This type of FDI generates benefits, but also comes with risks such as the emergence of political income, uncontrolled resource exploitation or short-term FDI that will bring no beneficial effects with regards to long-term economics. This, is for example, the case reported by Broadman and Isik (2007), relating to speculative FDI, which aims to take advantage of the high GDP growth rates per capita of emerging economies (such as Brazil, Russia, India or China itself) without taking into account possible long-term negative effects.

1.2.2. Policy trends of the host country that promote FDI

According to Cho (2003), policies for attracting FDI in most developed and developing countries have recently taken on a more liberal approach. This liberalisation at the heart of the policy aims to reduce barriers (e.g. customs or bureaucratic), improve the treatment of foreign investors and ensure that the markets are open to a wide range of investors. The liberalisation of the markets creates a more competitive market and forces many countries to exert greater effort in order to attract FDI by, for example, making labour or importation of labour policies more flexible (Broadman and Isik, 2007).

FDI is considered one of the largest sources of capitalisation of technical know-how. It is necessary to attract this source of capital not only to the industrial sector, but also to the services and extractive industry sectors.

This liberalisation brings with it an increase in options relating to the allocation of FDI.

Taking into account the measures employed by countries in order to attract investment, we see as a result a wide range of policy options:

- Create a sound and stable macro-economic environment, including a transparent business environment;

- Promotion of clusters and technical and physical infrastructure;
- Human resource development;
- Capacity development of local businesses, especially SMEs;
- Resolve social and environmental problems;
- Adoption of competitive laws and the reduction of practices restrictive to business;
- Influence the behaviour of investors through incentives and the imposing of performance requirements;
- Create larger markets through regional and bilateral cooperation;
- Investment protection, including copyright.

Several countries have implemented measures aimed at attracting FDI, which have evolved over the years to attract quality rather than quantity, focusing on benefiting the domestic economy.

With regards to the performance and efficiency requirements of FDI, almost all developed or developing countries have resorted to these requirements in order to achieve a certain level of development. Some of the specific targets of these requirements, according to Aguiar and Gula-mhussen (2009), are as follows:

- Deepening and broadening of the industrial base;
- Job creation;
- Promoting of trade links;
- Exportation generation and performance;
- Balance of economic transaction;
- Regional development promotion;
- Avoidance of restrictive business practices;
- Transfer of technology.

Strong local firms attract FDI and in turn the entry of foreign affiliates which increases the competitiveness and dynamism of the domestic market.

The strongest channels for diffusing skills, knowledge and technology are links formed with local businesses. These links can lead to business sector growth and provide a foundation for economic development.

Foreign companies, in turn, can benefit from these connections as they provide an opportunity to reduce costs and increase access to the local market; thus, there is substantial mutual interest in creating these ties.

Although there are various measures and policies in place with the aim of increasing the benefits generated from the investment, many of these measures were subject to a set of international rules proposed by the WTO (World Trade Organisation).

1.3. Factors that influence decisions of the investor

We will now study some factors that influence the decisions and behaviour of investors in order to find some elements that will allow us to explain why the Chinese are investing in Africa.

According to the article titled "Foreign Direct Investment in Africa", Ntwala Mwilima (2003),it is well known that a strong policy and regulatory regime, appropriate institutions, good infrastructure and political and economic stability are all important factors with regards to attracting investment.

According to Ludger Odenthal (2001), there are other determinants relating to investment abroad:

- International agreements relating to FDI;
- Economic determinants such as market size and per capita income;
- Economic determinants that attract FDI relating to natural resources;
- Economic determinants that attract FDI relating to efficiency;
- And privatisation programmes.

There are several mentioned reasons that justify the delay of FDI towards African countries, namely bureaucracy (as stated by Addison and Mavrotas, 2004), market size, lack of policies, lack of profit opportunities, negative perceptions, lack of implementation capacity, regulation in the work place, corruption and poor infrastructure. However, following the consideration of recent data showing an alarming depletion of Chinese ecosystems and primary sector resources, authors such as Alden (2009) state that the potential for resource exploitation (soil and subsoil) in Africa can be considered an element that attracts Chinese FDI.

If, in addition, we consider population growth in Africa, and the implied market growth, we can easily conclude that the reason for the evolution of FDI in Africa is also due to demographic stimulus.

Table 5 - Economic conditions and policies of receiving
countries that influence FDI

Economic Conditions	Markets	Size, income levels, urbanisation, prospects for stability and growth, accessibility to regional markets.
	Resources	Natural resources, location
	Competitiveness	Labour availability, cost, manpower capabilities, training capacity, capacity of management technicians, technical support, access to inputs, infrastructure.
Policies of host countries	Macro policies	Management of key macro variables, access to foreign exchange markets
	Private sector	Promoting the private sector, clear and stable policies, free entry and exit policies, efficient financial markets
	Industrial exchanges	Trade policy, regional integration and access to regional markets, competitiveness policies, support for small and medium-sized enterprises.
	FDI policies	Easy access, right to property, incentives, access to inputs, stable policies and transparency.

Source: Cho (2003)

According to Cho (2003), we can still conclude that FDI is usually a long-term commitment for the host country and contributes to capital formation in developing countries. As has been discussed in previous subchapters, this investment tends to be safer than other forms of raising capital as it generates obligations for the 'host' country; thus we have a higher level of stability. This means of financing / investment can be a valid instrument for developing countries as it means they can respond to opportunities that may arise during the integration of the global economy and thus compete in the global market.

Table 5 provides an overview of the political and economic conditions that influence the foreign investor. This table shows that there are two important factors: economic, which is divided into three conditions (Markets, Resources and Competitiveness); and political, which is divided into the four important factors of macro policies, FDI Policies, Private Sector, and Industrial Exchanges.

1.4. Conclusions derived from reviewing the literature

Following on from this series of subchapters, is now possible to form a general summary of the variables which may impact Chinese FDI allocated in Africa. The sited authors indicate the following dimensions and variables with regards to Chinese FDI, as shown in Table 6.

Table 6 - Summary of the determinants of Chinese FDI

Variables	Justification	Authors
Inflation	High inflation rates suggest greater macro-economic uncertainty	Bellak, Leibrecht and Stehrer (2008)
Corruption control	Less corruption promotes greater diversity of foreign investment	Aguiar and Gulamhussen (2009)
Government Efficiency	A more efficient government is less dependent on a single investor and single investment	Aguiar and Gulamhussen (2009)
Stability Policy	Greater political stability attracts investment	Aguiar and Gulamhussen (2009)
Growth of GDP per capita	Measure economic development causes	Broadman and Isik (2007)
GDP per capita	Scale effect in attracting FDI	Broadman and Isik (2007)
Population	Market effect	Acemoglu (2009)
Regulatory Quality	Clear laws attract FDI	Acemoglu (2009)
Forest area	Attraction by way of natural resources	Alden (2009)
Arable area	Attraction by way of natural resources	Alden (2009)
Index of export diversification	Investment attraction	Hung (2006)

Global FDI received	Pull effect (higher FDI issued by several countries leads to others investing in the receiving country)	Addison and Mavrotas (2004)
FDI (% GDP)	Composition effect (greater de-pendence on FDI tends to lead to future growth of FDI)	Addison and Mavrotas (2004)

2

Empirical Model and Data

2.1. Empirical model

Based on the literature review we saw in the first two chapters we will now draw up our econometric model:

$$idechines_{it} = const_{it} + \alpha 1 * idechines_{it-1} + \alpha 2 * corrupt_{it} + \alpha 3 * pop_{it} + \alpha 4 * forest_{it} +$$
$$\alpha 5 * govefi_{it} + \alpha 6 * polestab_{it} + \alpha 7 * \exp div_{it} + \alpha 8 * fdi_{it}$$
$$+ \alpha 9 * areaagric_{it} + \alpha 10 * gdppc_{it} + \alpha 11 * gdpgrow_{it} + \alpha 12 * \inf lat_{it} + ei + \varepsilon_{it}$$

Our econometric model will test the dimensions that will determine Chinese FDI allocated to 48 African countries observed between 2003 and 2008; a database can be found attached for reference purposes.

In EQ1, we estimate Foreign Direct Investment (idechines) to i (48) African countries between the period 2003-2008 (t), depending on the previous year's investment (ide_it-l), the level of corruption control (*corrupt_it*), population number (*pop_it*), the area covered by forest (*forest_it*), government efficiency (*govefi_it*), the level of political stability (*polestab_it*), the country's export diversification value (*expdiv_it*), the value of foreign direct investment (*fdi_it*), the size of the country's agricultural area (*areaagric_it*), GDP per capita (*gdppc_it*), the annual

GDP growth percentage (*gdpgrow_it*), the inflation growth percentage (*inflat_it*) and a constant (*const_it*).

For this study, the EQ1 is estimated by the GMM (Generalised Method of Moments), as this solution allows us to overcome autocorrelation problems more easily than by using other models.

Our observations panel consisted of 48 countries (see page 60) observed between 2003 and 2008. A text supporting the use of GMM can be found in Annex 3.

Table 7 below shows the sources of the variables that were used to build the database.

Table 7 - Sources of variables

Variable	Source
Chinese FDI	2008 Statistical Bulletin of China's Outward FDI
Population	World Bank Data
Surface area (kmA2)	World Bank Data
Forest area (sq. km)	World Bank Data
Corruption control	The Worldwide Governance Indicators (WGI) project
Government efficiency	The Worldwide Governance Indicators (WGI) project
Political stability	The Worldwide Governance Indicators (WGI) project
Quality regulator (0-100%)	The Worldwide Governance Indicators (WGI) project
Diversification of exports index	World Bank Data
FDI net inflows (USD)	World Bank Data
FDI (% of GDP)	World Bank Data
Agricultural area (sq km)	World Bank Data
Time needed to open a business (years)	World Bank Data
GDP per capita (USD)	World Bank Data
Growth of per capita GDP (annual%)	World Bank Data
Inflation	World Bank Data

2.2. Results

Table 8 shows the descriptive statistics of the variables.

TABLE 8 - Descriptive statistics

Variables	Comments	Average	Detour	Maximum	Minimum
Inflation, GDP deflator (annual%)	273	1,972	1,096	5,943	-3.538
corruption control	288	3,142	0.935	4,437	0
Government efficiency	288	2,975	1,039	4,431	-0.105
Political stability	282	3,239	0.931	4,483	-0.336
Growth GDP per capita (GDP per capita growth) -% annual	229	1,112	0.912	3,533	-2.534
GDP per capita (current USD)	285	6,737	1,236	10.244	4,449
Population	288	15.881	1,518	18.835	11,321
regulatory quality (percentile rank 0-100)	287	3,105	0.886	4,372	-0.693
Forest area (KmA2)	240	10,091	2,503	14.11	3,784
Agriculture (KmA2)	240	2,023	2,023	14.129	4,094
Export diversification index	240	1,668	1,069	4,278	0.095
Foreign Direct Investment (% of GDP)	214	18.687	2,233	23.172	8,433
Starting a business (time in years)	180	1,117	0.414	2,079	0.262
Chinese FDI	277	2,536	2,023	8,024	-4.605

Some of the variables (GDP per capita, population, forest area, agricultural area and Chinese FDI) were "logarithmic" in order to avoid the risk of heteroscedasticity problems when formulating the table

Below is displayed the table of results (Table 9).

TABLE 9 - Results (Generalised Method of Moments)

Variables	(1)	(2)	(3)	(4)	(5)	(6)	(7)	(8)	(9)
Chinese FDI (previous year)	-0.199*	0.305***	0.394***	0.395	0.357***	0.358***	0.372***	0.352***	0.401***
	(0.204)	(0.115)	(0.129)	(0.123)	(0.123)	(0.125)	(0.122)	(0.124)	(0.11)
GDP growth per capita (annual%)	0.123***	0.17**	0.264**	0.266***	0.179	0.188	0.186	0,193*	0.159*
	(0.472)	(0.157)	(0.137)	(0.138)	(0.118)	(0.12)	(0.121)	(0.115)	(0.096)
Corruption control	-0.095*	0.401**	0.915*	0.912*	1,083***	0.901	0.873**	0.804**	0.568
	(0.335)	(0.324)	(0.487)	(0.485)	(0.417)	(0.362)	(0.397)	(0.379)	(0.356)
Government efficiency	-0.878***	-0.703***	-0.697*	-0.71*	-0.656*	-0.698**	-0.683**	-0.653**	-0.558*
	(0.212)	(0.268)	(0.397)	(0.403)	(0.346)	(0.335)	(0.342)	(0.329)	(0.329)
Stability Policy	0.626*	0.727*	0.902	·0.893*	0.922*	0.94**	0.967**	0.976**	0.977**
	(0.364)	(0.389)	(0.569)	(0.523)	(0.478)	(0.464)	(0.473)	(0.464)	(0.434)
Inflation, GDP deflator (annual%)	-0.047	0.315**	0.311	0.314	0.139**	0.149	0.169	0.183	
	(0.111)	(0.313)	(0.229)	(0.248)	(0.177)	(0.172)	(0.178)	(0.177)	
GDP per capita (current US $)	0.742**	1,101	2,163**	2.143·**	1,026	0.867	0.605		
	(0.657)	(0.802)	(0.987)	(0.986)	(0.666)	(0.57)	(0.588)		
Population	-19.231**	-16.342*	-16.753	-15.698*	-9.914	-10.215			
	(9,001)	(8,916)	(11,214)	(9,153)	(7,236)	(7,171)			

Regulatory quality (percentile rank 0-100)	0.225*	0.605	-0.254*	-0.241**	-0.574				
	(0.486)	(0.572)	(0.533)	(0.549)	(0.483)				
Forest area (sq. Km)	-3.996**	-4.605**	-1.564	-1.366*					
	(3.925)	(1.963)	(11.21)	(3.539)					
Agricultural area (sq. km)	0.001**	-0.001	3.235*						
	(0.001)	(0.001)	(16.965)						
FDI net inflows (current US $)	-0.063**	0.127*							
	(0.055)	(0.202)							
Export diversification index	-0.031*								
	(0.335)								
Constant	0.839	0.507	0.367	0.355	0.363	0.376	0.183	0.279	0.289
	(0, 23)	(0.234)	(0.241)	(0.209)	(0.2)	(0.197)	(0.123)	(0.075)	(0.68)
Wald statist	205.59	34.29	36.99	35.88	26.2	21.96	16.55	14.69	24.93
Arellano-Bond test of 2nd autocorrelation	-1.16	-0.58	0.23	0.23	0.96	0.65	1.1	1.04	0.56
Number of observations	58	77	90	90	123	123	123	123	126
Number of groups	29	35	39	39	41	41	41	41	41

Legend: significance level of 1% (***); 5% (**); 10% (*). Estimated errors in brackets

It is now possible to analyse the results obtained by our econometric model shown in the previous table. It is possible to conclude, from taking into account the available data, that the Chinese Direct Investment level of the previous period, Corruption Control Level, the Government Efficiency of the African country, the political stability of the country, and the percentage growth of the African country's GDP are the factors that have the most impact on Chinese Direct Investment.

Now that we know the variables that are most important for Chinese investment in Africa but we still need to consider what impact these have, that is, if the impact is positive or negative. The variables that have a positive impact are: Chinese investment in the previous period, control of the level of corruption, political stability and the percentage growth of GDP. The only negative factor corresponds to the efficiency of the government.

We can now quantify the impact these have on the FDI, using the results obtained for the most parsimonious specification:

- If the previous year's FDI grew 1%, Chinese FDI this year will increase by 0.4%;
- If the corruption control level of increased by 1%, Chinese FDI will by increase 0.56%;
- If political stability grew by 1%, Chinese FDI will grow in turn by 0.97%;
- If the growth of GDP per capita increased by 1 percentage point, Chinese FDI will grow 0.15%;
- If the Government's efficiency grew by 1%, Chinese FDI will decrease by -0.5%.

2.3. Implications

Taking into account the results obtained in our study, it was concluded that for Chinese investors, the most important variables are directly linked to the political level and economic growth of the country, namely: Chinese Direct Investment of the previous period, the corruption control level, the African country's government efficiency, political stability and the percentage growth of the African country's GDP.

The variables that have a positive impact are: Chinese investment in the previous period, corruption level control, political stability and the GDP percentage growth, leading us to conclude that the improvement of these variables is in the best interests of Chinese investors and thus the countries receiving the investment also. It is suggested then, that these same countries should implement policies that favour, to a large extent, these components of its political-economic environment, such as policies aimed at political stability and corruption control or, from a political or economic point of view, that lead to an increase in GDP.

The only negative variable observed is the government's efficiency level. This can be interpreted in various ways, for example, being a more efficient government requires fewer resources to meet the same objectives, a more efficient government can lead to greater difficulty with regards to reaching an investment agreement; a more efficient government has already attracted other investors or is inclined to be interested in a different level of investment.

In summary, the variables that have a positive effect are: Chinese investment in the previous period, corruption level control, political stability and the GDP percentage growth; this leads us to conclude that the improvement of these variables is in the best interests of Chinese investors and thus the countries receiving the investment also.

3

Conclusion

This work addressed the issue of Chinese Foreign Direct Investment (FDI) in Africa and more specifically addressed the variables that determine Chinese FDI in Africa.

The first chapters covered the more general issues and outlined the theme and basic concepts in order to better understand the work. The second chapter, following on from the literature review summary, shows examples of variables used and authors that support them.

The third chapter discussed the model used to estimate the determinants of the equation. This equation was estimated by the Generalised Method of Moments (GMM).

From the results it was concluded that the most important variables for Chinese investors are linked directly to the political and economic growth levels of the African country. Then going into more detail, the most attractive variables for Chinese investors in Africa were shown to be: Chinese Direct Investment during the previous period, corruption level control, political stability and the GDP growth percentage of the African country.

Higher levels of government efficiency were shown to correlate negatively with Chinese FDI amounts, leading us to conclude that the higher the degree of efficiency, the lower the FDI amount.

Based on the results, an economic policy of African governments aiming to generate a continuum of Chinese FDI, should promote the following initiatives:

- Increase the quality of national political institutions;
- Encourage economic growth or more specifically, boost economic growth rates;
- Reduce the level of corruption perceived by investors;
- Increase the country's political stability.

However, as it we have seen that the most efficient governments are less dependent on Chinese FDI, we can conclude that policies leading to more efficient public practice may reduce the typical problems experienced by African governments, namely the dependence on foreign mono- investors or foreign mono-investment.

Exhibits

This Annex corresponds to the database formulated by the author of this work relative to the 48 countries under review.

ANNEX 1

Database

Countries	Year	Chinese FDI	Population	Surface area (Km "2)	Forestry Area (K "2)	Corruption control	Government Efficiency	Political stability	Regulatory quality (percentile rank 0-100)
Algeria	2003	5.70	31885164	2381740	22237	35.4	30.8	4.8	29.8
	2004	34.49	32365777		22503	33	39.8	8.7	26.8
	2005	171.21	32854159		22768	41.3	43.6	15.4	29.8
	2006	247.37	33351137		23034	41.3	39.3	16.3	24.9
	2007	393.89	33852675.6		23299	43.5	35.1	13.9	25.2
	2008	508.82	34361756.4			40.6	37	13.4	21.3
Angola	2003	00:30	15646832	1246700	593536	6.8	10	15.9	9.3
	2004	00:47	16135465		592,288	6.8	8.5	19.2	10.7
	2005	8.79	16617589		591 040	8.7	12.8	22.6	8.3
	2006	37.23	17089111		589792	7.8	9.5	29.3	13.2
	2007	78.46	17554585		588,544	6.8	11.8	28.4	16.5
	2008	68.89	18020668			6.3	13.7	29.7	16.9
Benin	2003	7.71	7358142	112620	24806	32	44.1	57.7	31.7
	2004	20:51	7610730		24158	35.4	38.4	47.6	34.1
	2005	19	7867626		23510	18	32.2	57.2	32.7
	2006	22:12	8128208		22862	34	32.7	57.2	36.6
	2007	35.60	8393132		22214	42.5	32.2	57.2	32.5
	2008	53.15	8662086			42	35.5	57.4	35.7
Botswana	2003	2.70	1795203	581,730	121798	84.5	75.4	81.7	74.6
	2004	3.80	1815097		120,614	81.6	74.9	80.3	70.2
	2005	18:12	1835938		119430	83	74.9	82.2	67.8
	2006	25.52	1858163		118,246	77.7	71.6	80.3	65.9
	2007	43.39	1881431.526		117 062	78.3	73.5	81.7	65
	2008	65.26	1904991.428			80.2	73.5	81.3	67.1

Exports diversification index	Foreign direct investment, net inflows (current USD)	Foreign direct investment (% of GDP)	Forestry area (Km^2)	Open a business, (time in years)	GDP per capita (current USD)	GDP growth per capita - % Yearly	Inflation, GDP deflator (annual%)
3.1	633800000.00		399 057		2133.24	5.32	8.32
2.3	881900000.00		411,450	2.5	2626.66	3.64	10.63
2.4	1,081,300,000.00		412,110	2.5	3114.95	3.54	16.46
2.3	1,795,400,000.00		411,810	2.5	3491.95	0.48	10.61
2.4	1,664,600,000.00		412,520	2.5	3967.31	1.47	6.79
				2.5	5060.32	1.47	17.16
1.1	3,504,701,780.00	24.94	575,900		891.95	0.12	102.54
1.1	1,449,230,000.00	7.15	575,900	6.2	1225.57	7.82	42.71
1.1	1,303,840,000.00	-4.97	575,900	6.2	1843.37	17.11	33.99
1.1	37,710,000.00	-0.51	575,900	6.2	2642.81	15.29	14.66
1.1	893340000.00	-3.05	575,900	6.2	3375.95	17.09	4.13
				6.2	4627.10	11.83	19.89
4.2	44.732.0 00.00	1.25	34,670		483.54	0.44	1.72
3.9	63,840,000.00	1.61	35,670	4	531.81	-0.32	0.29
4.8	53,040,000.00	1.25	35,670	4	544.95	-0.46	2.79
6.3	53,200,481.94	1.19	35,170	4	568.81	0.47	2.99
6.4	48,000,000.00		35,200	4	646.67	1.30	2.87
				4	771.18	1.84	9.42
1.3	417996331.61	2.56	257,960		4610.94	5.10	2.68
1.4	390970000.00	3.68	258,270	2.2	5414.27	5.37	5.65
1.4	278590000.00	3.18	258,415	2.2	5725.96	3.50	11.28
1.8	486390000.00	4.87	258,420	2.2	5923.30	1.73	16.14
2.8	28,560,000.00	-0.26	258,520	1.7	6550.23	2.96	12.97
				1.7	6808.01	-2.22	17.17

Countries	Year	Chinese FDI	Population	Surface area (Km "2)	Forestry Area (K "2)	Corruption control	Government Efficiency	Political stability	Regulatory quality (percentile rank 0-100)
Burundi	2003		6955720	27830	1704	16	5.7	2.9	11.2
	2004	00:02	7162083		1612	16	6.2	1.4	11.2
	2005		7378129		1520	17.5	7.6	9.6	9.8
	2006	1.65	7603492		1428	9.7	10	9.6	10.7
	2007	4.65	7837981		1336	10.1	7.6	11.1	10.7
	2008	5:13	8074254			15.9	10.4	10	12.1
Cameroon	2003	5.73	17018907	475440	216850	21.4	23.2	26.9	19.5
	2004	6.98	17409433		214,650	12.6	18	24.5	29.3
	2005	7.87	17795149		212450	10.7	15.6	31.7	23.4
	2006	16:46	18174696		210250	13.6	16.6	32.7	23.4
	2007	18:51	18,532,798.56		208050	15.5	17.1	31.3	24.3
	2008	20:34	18,897,956.94			18.8	19.9	27.8	26.1
Cape Verde	2003		462440	4030	830	65	58.3	80.8	46.3
	2004	00:01	470 028		833	62.1	58.3	86.1	43.9
	2005	00:01	47743 8		836	66.5	54.5	68.8	48.3
	2006	4:05	484,659		842	71.4	61.6	81.7	49.8
	2007	4:05	491717		845	74.4	65.9	80.3	49
	2008	5:13	498,672			75.4	57.3	76.1	53.1
Central Africa	2003		4059572	623,000	228,142	8.3	3.3	10.1	9.8
	2004		4123325		227846	7.3	3.3	12	9.3
	2005	2.00	4191429		227550	9.7	2.8	14.9	7.8
	2006	3.98	4264806		227254	15	3.3	5.8	9.3
	2007	3.98	4343404.857		226958	18.4	4.7	6.7	9.7
	2008	3.98	4423452.264			18.4	3.3	6.7	8.7
Chad	2003		9465233	1284000	120794	8.7	14.7	31.7	17.1
	2004		9810218		120002	9.2	11.8	31.3	20
	2005	2.71	10145609		119210	4.4	10	7.2	13.7
	2006	12.78	10468179		118418	6.8	5.7	23.1	12.7
	2007	13:53	10,763,638.42		117,626	5.3	3.8	27.9	12.1
	2008	25.36	11,067,437.03			3.4	2.8	39.7	9.2

Exports diversification index	Foreign direct investment, net inflows (current USD)	Foreign direct investment (% of GDP)	Forestry area (Km^2)	Open a business, (time in years)	GDP per capita (current USD)	GDP growth per capita - % Yearly	Inflation, GDP deflator (annual %)
2.8	4,600.00	0.00	23,300		85.54	-3.91	11.55
3.4	40,000.00	0.01	23,050		92.78	1.81	8.33
2	580.000,00	0.07	22,860		107.87	-2.05	16.62
5.4	30,000.00	0.00	22,900		120.84	2.01	4.42
2.6	500,000.00	0.05	22,950		125.00	0.50	8.28
					144.04	1.44	24.49
4.7	219753838.66	2.52	91,600		800.39	1.64	0.36
4	85,580,000.00	0.53	91,600	3.2	906.14	1.38	1.51
4.1	244360000.00	1.61	91,600	3.2	932.16	0.08	2.63
3	16,380,000.00	0.36	91,600	3.2	988.02	1.07	3.94
3.3	433100000.00	2.85	91,600	3.2	1116.48	1.50	2.06
				3.2	1238.02	1.89	1.69
14.5	39,255,000.00	4.82	770		1724.15	4.42	1.60
13.6	67,590,000.00	7.31	770		1967.21	-2.32	6.17
7.9	16,700,000.00	7.99	770		2107.86	4.88	2.01
10	122600000.00	10.97	780		2479.34	9.15	6.83
9	130290000.00	13.24	780		2941.85	5.41	3.18
					3468.42	4.47	5.44
5.4	3269098.42		51,950		280.62	-9.01	-1.33
5.5	15,107,000.00		52,150	4.8	307.91	-0.56	0.30
4.7	17,107,000.00		52,150	4.8	322.10	0.74	3.68
4.6	18,107,000.00		51,900	4.8	346.29	2.21	4.27
5.5	27,207,000.00		52,050	4.8	394.20	2.31	1.98
				4.8	445.39	0.94	4.59
2.2	712654852.03		488,300		289.13	10.52	0.08
1.4	495376548.64		488,300		450.04	28.93	9.73
1.7	612928177.63		492,300		578.90	4.37	23.06
1.2	700,000,000.00		493,300		601.80	-2.93	6.17
1.1	602768242.09		493,300		650.90	-2.55	1.74
					755.43	-3.13	11.94

Countries	Year	Chinese FDI	Population	Surface area (Km "2)	Forestry Area (K "2)	Corruption control	Government Efficiency	Political stability	Regulatory quality (percentile rank 0-100)
Cameroon	2003		575660	1861	65	22.8	4.7	29.3	5.9
	2004	00:01	587943.7126		60	22.3	3.8	49	5.9
	2005	00:01	600489.541		55	21.4	1.9	41.3	5.9
	2006	4:05	6 613 5.9773 0		49	32	1.4	39.4	6.3
	2007	4:05	628410.0607		44	29	1.4	18.3	6.3
	2008	4:05	643571.3128			25.6	1.4	15.3	4.3
DR Congo	2003	00:24	55174963	2344860	1342483	1.9	2.8		3.9
	2004	15.69	56917959		1339289	3.4	2.4		3.4
	2005	25.11	58740547		1336095	2.4	1.4		4.4
	2006	37.61	60643890		1332901	2.4	0.9		7.3
	2007	104.40	62,399,224.14		1329707	3.9	0.9		8.3
	2008	134.14	64,205,366.34			5.3	0.9		5.3
Congo	2003		3260769	30350	225053	13.6	5.2	8.7	15.1
	2004	5.65	3341052		224883	16.5	9	10.6	16.1
	2005	13:32	3416654		224,713	14.1	6.2	8.2	10.7
	2006	62.90	3486073		224543	11.7	6.2	15.9	13.7
	2007	65.40	3551105		224373	10.6	5.2	19.2	11.2
	2008	75.42	3615152			7.7	8.1	24.9	11.6
Ivory Coast	2003	8:05	18453355	322460	103,742	13.1	15.6	4.3	22.9
	2004	14:10	18839434		103896	8.7	7.1	1.9	15.6
	2005	29.11	19244866		104050	7.3	4.7	1.4	16.6
	2006	37.61	19673411		104204	6.3	4.3	1.9	19
	2007	104.40	20122796		104358	8.2	5.7	3.8	18
	2008	134.14	20591302			7.2	6.6	5.3	17.4
Djibouti	2003		776,784	23200	56	22.8	22.7	21.2	21
	2004	00:40	790,344		56	40.3	29.4	38	21
	2005	00:40	804,206		56	31.6	19.9	26.4	21
	2006	0.60	818,508		56	33	13.3	38.5	21
	2007	1.60	832991.9902		56	40.1	15.2	41.8	21.4
	2008	1.60	847732.2832			45.4	14.2	37.8	22.2

Exports diversification index	Foreign direct investment, net inflows (current USD)	Foreign direct investment (% of GDP)	Forestry area (Km^2)	Open a business, (time in years)	GDP per capita (current USD)	GDP growth per capita - % Yearly	Inflation, GDP deflator (annual %)
1.7	1,000,000.00		1,470		563.65	0.33	5.13
2.4	671354.37		1,480		616.42	-2.32	1.77
4.6	558643.68		1,480		644.54	2.05	2.30
5.6	576283.63		1,500		657.06	-0.92	2.00
4.9	800,000.00		1,500		739.88	-1.88	5.18
					823.70	-1.40	5.50
3.4	323129731.59		228,000		102.82	2.65	13.04
4	9920000.00		228,000	5.2	115.86	3.37	6.51
4.7	76,030,000.00		228,000	5.2	123.23	4.54	21.79
6.2	115980000.00		226,500	5.2	144.87	2.27	13.58
7.6	720000000.00		226,500	5.2	159.45	3.27	17.68
				5.2	180,49	3.21	19.47
1.6	323124395.36	9.02	105,450		1093.05	-0.81	-3.25
1.5	8520000.00	-0.30	105,450	3	1299.87	1.11	6.91
1.4	1,809,970,000.00	8.44	105,450	3	1781.57	5.32	29.94
1.3	2,890,280,000.00	19.24	105,450	3	2217.76	4.12	18.52
1.4	4,289,470,000.00	34.51	105,450	3	2153.09	-3.39	-7.89
				3	2959.49	3.70	23.85
4.8	165347467.49	1.20	195,000		744.44	-3.57	1.30
7.2	282980000.00	1.83	199,000	2.2	821.74	-0.29	0.63
7.1	311920000.00	1.91	200,000	2.2	850.28	-0.88	4.23
7.7	318860000.00	1.84	202,000	2.2	882.78	-1.51	4.50
7.7	426900000.00	2,16	202,000	2.2	983.75	-0.56	2.71
				2.2	1137.08	-0.11	8.12
13.1	14,224,542.96	2.29	17,010		800.79	1.34	1.97
15	38,540,000.00	5.79	17,010	5	842.76	2.05	3.13
44.6	22,200,000.00	3.13	17,010		881.42	1.39	3.15
23.9	108290000.00	14.24	17,013	5	929.32	2.29	3.08
5.9	195351140.27	23.89	17,013	5	981.62	2.45	3.10
				5	1031.80	2.05	3.09

Countries	Year	Chinese FDI	Population	Surface area (Km "2)	Forestry Area (K "2)	Corruption control	Government Efficiency	Political stability	Regulatory quality (percentile rank 0-100)
Egypt	2003	14:29	74296319	1001450	638	41.7	45	24	33.7
	2004	14:28	75718360		654	41.3	45.5	21.2	36.1
	2005	39.80	77154409		670	40.8	38.9	19.7	37.1
	2006	100.43	78602081		686	37.9	33.2	21.2	34.6
	2007	131.60	80060540		702	36.7	40.3	25	42.2
	2008	31.35	81527172			29.5	43.1	23	49.3
Equatorial Guinea	2003	8.64	576342	28050	16625	2.4	9.5	38	7.3
	2004	10:21	592,466		16473	1	5.7	37.5	6.8
	2005	16:56	608807		16320	1	6.6	35.6	7.3
	2006	30.44	625,394		16167	1.5	6.6	43.3	7.8
	2007	44.63	642,210		16015	2.4	6.2	43.3	7.8
	2008	40.62	659,197			1.9	4.3	40.2	6.8
Eritrea	2003	1.88	4175647	117600	15628	54.9	16.1	24.5	7.8
	2004	00:12	4353526		15584	49.5	10.4	26	4.4
	2005	00:12	4526722		15540	47.6	14.7	23.1	2.4
	2006	6.63	4692115		15540	46.6	8.1	18.3	2.4
	2007	7:22	4841772.662		15496	35.3	8.5	16.8	2.4
	2008	6.73	4996203.739			43.5	4.7	19.6	1.9
Ethiopia	2003	4.78	70880658	1104300	132820	31.6	17.1	12	13.7
	2004	7.87	72746225		131410	27.7	24.6	13.5	16.6
	2005	29.82	74660901		130000	24.3	16.6	7.7	16.1
	2006	95.60	76627697		128590	31.1	30.3	6.7	19.5
	2007	108.88	78646128		127180	27.5	39.8	7.2	19.4
	2008	126.45	80713434			30.4	39.8	6.2	19.8
Gabon	2003	24.05	1315994	267,670	217954	40.3	35.5	53.4	49.3
	2004	31.27	1342701		217852	29.1	22.3	52.9	35.6
	2005	35.36	1369229		21775 0	33.5	28	51.9	42
	2006	51.28	1395613		217648	18	26.5	48.6	32.7
	2007	55.59	1421882		217,546	19.8	28	50.5	31.6
	2008	88.14	1448159			12.1	26.1	52.6	27.5

Exports diversification index	Foreign direct investment, net inflows (current USD)	Foreign direct investment (% of GDP)	Forestry area (Km^2)	Open a business, (time in years)	GDP per capita (current USD)	GDP growth per capita - % Yearly	Inflation, GDP deflator (annual %)
22.1	237400000.00	0.26	34,090		1116.12	1.26	6.76
22	1,253,300,000.00	1.39	34,780	4.2	1041.30	2,12	11.68
22.6	5.375.6 0 0000.00	5.89	35,230	4.2	1162.42	2.53	6.21
14	10042800000.00	9.21	35,330	4.2	1367.45	4.88	7.36
17.2	11578100000.00	8.36	35,380	4.2	1629.71	5.12	12.61
				4.2	1997.10	5.14	12,30
1.2			3,240		5122.59	10.80	0.64
1.1			3,240		8845.81	34.24	16.92
1.2			3,240		13497.38	6.80	42.64
1.2			3,240		15355.42	-1.43	14.41
1.3			3,240		19582.02	18.26	-1.16
					28102.53	8.43	23.67
31.2	22,000,000.00		75,670		143.14	-6.76	16.57
27.8	7870000.00		75,000		144.99	-2.69	19.22
9.5	1,040,000.00		75,220		256.58	-1.35	35.63
22.4	450,000.00		75,520		273.17	-4.46	10.49
2.1	2820000.00		75,420		283.81	-1.81	5.86
					331.04	-1.15	18,00
4.6	465000000.00	0.00	316 070		120.71	-4.68	12.77
4.1	545000000.00	0.00	331,010	3	138.18	10.66	3.91
4.2	265110000.00	2.15	336,910	3	164.81	8.95	9.88
4.5	545260000.00	3.60	342,190	3	197.92	8.01	11.56
4.7	222590000.00	1.14	350,770	3	246.61	8.25	16.84
				3	328.16	8.47	29.07
1.7	157986838.29	2.95	51,600		4601.00	0.37	-0.09
1.8	319510000.00	4.80	51,600	5	5346.04	-0.67	6.33
1.7	242340000.00	1.93	51,600		6328.92	1.03	17,00
1.9	267805315.56		51,600	5	6839.99	-0.73	7.93
1.9	269324270.26		51,600	5	8135.41	3.60	5.22
				5	9967.80	0.21	14.25

Countries	Year	Chinese FDI	Population	Surface area (Km"2)	Forestry Area (K"2)	Corruption control	Government Efficiency	Political stability	Regulatory quality (percentile rank 0-100)
Gambia	2003	00:04	1436321	11300	4670	46.6	39.3	58.7	36.1
	2004	00:20	1481256		4690	32.5	36	56.3	39.5
	2005	1:19	1526138		4710	29.6	28.4	54.8	35.6
	2006	1:19	1570883		4730	28.2	24.6	44.7	38.5
	2007	1:19	1615510		4750	24.6	27.5	40.9	38.8
	2008	1:19	1660200			24.2	23.2	50.7	36.2
Ghana	2003	6.60	20954557	238540	57478	49.5	45.5	45.7	42
	2004	6:31	21435257		56324	48.1	44.1	46.2	42.4
	2005	7:33	21915168		55170	46.6	49.8	56.3	50.7
	2006	8:09	22393338		54016	58.3	52.6	55.8	54.1
	2007	41.87	22870966		52862	58.5	49.8	53.4	53.9
	2008	5802	23350927			56.5	52.1	46.9	54.6
Guinea Bissau	2003	14:34	8869959	245860	67962	24.8	17.5	28.4	13.2
	2004	25.77	9040537		67602	18.4	16.1	20.2	17.1
	2005	44.22	9220768		67242	18.9	11.8	16.8	18.5
	2006	54.63	9411881		66,882	14.1	4.7	6.3	15.6
	2007	69.97	9615073		66522	2.9	4.3	3.4	13.1
	2008	96.37	9833055			4.3	6.2	4.8	13.5
Kenya	2003	25.53	33779932	580370	35460	20.9	22.3	17.3	48.8
	2004	28.46	34674703		35340	20.9	24.2	17.3	44.4
	2005	58.25	35598952		35220	15.5	22.3	13.9	45.4
	2006	46.23	36553490		35100	18.4	28.4	16.8	42.4
	2007	55.13	37,530,725.66		34980	14.5	30.3	15.4	45.1
	2008	78.36	38,534,087.13			13.5	32.2	12	50.7
Lesotho	2003	00:24	19 4 9772	30350	76	46.1	44.5	52.9	29.3
	2004	00:03	1965823		78	50	47.9	61.1	27.8
	2005	0.60	1980831		80	54.9	47.9	56.7	28.8
	2006	7.60	1994888		82	57.3	40.3	51.9	30.7
	2007	7.60	2005825.716		84	52.7	41.7	42.3	26.7
	2008	8:22	2016823.401			59.9	46	43.1	28.5

Exports diversification index	Foreign direct investment, net inflows (current USD)	Foreign direct investment (% of GDP)	Forestry area (Km^2)	Open a business, (time in years)	GDP per capita (current USD)	GDP growth per capita - % Yearly	Inflation, GDP deflator (annual %)
8.2	21,902,464.96	5.97	7,740		255.63	3.53	27.39
10.7	56,750,000.00	14,15	7,990	3	270.72	3.80	12,20
6.1	51,930,000.00	11.26	7,940		302.27	2.02	4.14
5.2	82,070,000.00	16,17	8,100	3	323.17	3.52	1.44
6.6	68,450,000.00	10.64	8,130	3	398.33	3.37	5.69
				3	470.74	3.04	5.95
5.3	136750000.00	1.79	147,350		363.84	2.79	28.70
5.3	139270000.00	1.57	148,500	1.9	413.89	3.23	14,35
5.2	144970000.00	1.35	148,500	1.9	489.17	3.58	14.96
4.7	636010000.00	5.00	149,500	1.9	567.81	4.13	12.72
4.5	970380000.00	6.47	148,500	1.9	655.39	3.88	13.84
				1.9	690.48	4.02	18.02
3.5	78,966,000.00	2.18	129,600		408.06	0.15	11.11
3.3	98,000,000.00		130,650	3.8	435.63	0.77	20.98
3.1	105000000.00		132,700	3.8	353.61	1.31	28.60
3.4	108000000.00		134,700	3.8	340.41	0.09	37.39
3.2	111000000.00	8.46	135,700	3.8	474.63	-0.64	17.38
				3.8	433.86	6.00	38.87
18.8	81,738,242.64	0.53	268,740		441.20	0.29	6.20
18.4	46,060,000.00	0.26	269,920	4.5	464.07	2.38	7.11
17.9	21,210,000.00	0.06	270,020	4.5	527.23	3.05	5.21
19.9	50,670,000.00	0.12	270,540	4.5	614.95	3.62	7.42
21.9	727.730.00 0.00	2.57	270,000	4.5	718.09	4.18	4.65
				4.5	895.49	0.90	27,00
7.3	115714934.93	11.64	23,040		509.94	2.98	2.50
7.1	123490000.00	9.57	23,140	2.6	656.10	3.70	5.95
7.2	92,600,000.00	6.73	23,340	2.6	694.66	-0.08	4.31
7.9	113050000.00	7.45	23,040	2.6	760.70	7.34	8.56
6.6	130340000.00	7.81	23,040	2.6	832.36	4.49	9.16
				2.6	804.26	3.38	9.60

Countries	Year	Chinese FDI	Population	Surface area (Km "2)	Forestry Area (K "2)	Corruption control	Government Efficiency	Political stability	Regulatory quality (percentile rank 0-100)
Liberia	2003	5.80	3137852	111370	32744	7.3	1.9	1.4	3.4
	2004	6:38	3224643		32142	7.8	1.4	7.7	2.4
	2005	15.95	3334222		31540	11.7	8.1	9.1	4.9
	2006	29.51	3471020		30938	29.6	8.5	11.5	6.8
	2007	29.78	3627285		30336	44.4	10.4	10.1	9.2
	2008	37.36	3793400			33.3	7.6	17.2	7.7
Libya	2003	0.86	5682648	1759540	2170	26.7	19.4	37.5	4.9
	2004	0.87	5799484		2170	24.8	26.1	46.6	10.2
	2005	33.06	5918217		2170	25.7	20.4	52.4	00 00
	2006	28.57	6038643		2170	21.8	27	53.8	00 00
	2007	70.83	6156487.535		2170	24.2	16.1	60.6	17.5
	2008	146.52	6276631.814			21.7	18	63.2	17.9
Madagascar	2003	28.13	16656727	587 040	129119	59.2	37.4	60.1	44.9
	2004	40.63	17131317		128749	54.9	43.6	51.9	41.5
	2005	49.94	17614261		128378	55.8	47.4	44.7	42.4
	2006	54.34	18105439		128,007	49.5	37.9	48.1	45.4
	2007	76.01	18604365		127637	55.6	42.7	42.8	47.1
	2008	146.52	19110941			55.1	33.2	30.1	41.5
Malawi	2003	0.72	12573672	118,480	34680	24.3	27	40.9	38
	2004	0.72	12893865		34350	25.2	23.2	42.3	32.2
	2005	0.73	13226091		34020	22.8	27.5	51	32.2
	2006	0.96	13570713		33690	27.2	19.4	46.6	27.3
	2007	1:16	13,920,061.89		33360	25.6	36.5	43.8	35.4
	2008	6:59	142 784 04,02			33.8	30.3	46.4	38.6
Mali	2003	12:59	10929518	1240190	127715	38 3	39 8	47 6	37.1
	2004	13:16	11264724		126715	44.7	33.6	56.7	37.6
	2005	13:28	11611090		125,715	45.6	33.2	49	38.5
	2006	19.83	11968376		124,715	40.8	29.9	43.8	40.5
	2007	32.22	12,334,168.03		123,715	46.4	31.8	38.9	42.7
	2008	30.95	12,711,139.84			37.7	21.8	35.9	40.6

Exports diversification index	Foreign direct investment, net inflows (current USD)	Foreign direct investment (% of GDP)	Forestry area (Km^2)	Open a business, (time in years)	GDP per capita (current USD)	GDP growth per capita - % Yearly	Inflation, GDP deflator (annual %)
3.1	372220000.00		25,900		130.73	-33.07	2.65
3.4	69,270,000.00	15.06	25,950	3	142.65	-0.16	1.07
3.3	75,830,000.00	14,30	25,950	3	159.02	1.84	13.83
5	107860000.00	17.63	26000		176.28	3.55	8.77
3.5	131640000.00	17.91	26000	3	202.61	4.69	15.96
				3	229.37	2.41	12.75
1.4		0.34	154,500		4192.13	-4.71	29.85
1.3		0.23	155,850		5258.76	2.88	23.07
1.3		2.18	155,850		7053.33	4.17	29.06
1.3		3.20	155,500		8232.10	3.10	13.69
1.3		6.72	155,500		9475.10	4.76	5.39
					15920.40	4.95	55.52
10.5	7442129.89	0.24	408,430		328.63	6.71	2.76
15.7	52,910,000.00	1.21	408,430		254.73	2.34	14,30
19.6	85,440,000.00	1.70	408,430		286.05	1.73	18,30
19.5	294216496.29		408,430		304.62	2.17	11.47
21.2	996883571.51		408,430		394.91	3.39	9.68
					469.36	4.05	9.62
3.2	3900000.00		48,200		192.84	3.63	8.75
3.8	107712000.00		49,700	2.6	203.60	3.05	14.51
2.9	26,500,000.00		49,700	2.6	215.86	-0.02	15,30
3	29,700,000.00		49,700	2.6	233.13	5.45	17.65
3.8	54,637,333.33		49,700	2.6	257.60	5.87	7.39
				2.6	298.98	6.95	8.95
1.5	132260768.22	3.00	396,790		399.14	4.27	1.28
1.3	101,000,000.00	2.06	390,390	3.6	432.69	-0.86	-0.61
1.5	223800000.00	4.24	393,890	3.6	456.92	2.92	2.45
2.9	83,390,000.00	1.40	394,390	3.6	490.13	2,16	4.09
2	360,000,000.00	0.96	396,190	3.6	555.20	-0.25	4.08
				3.6	687.61	1.89	13.58

Countries	Year	Chinese FDI	Population	Surface area (Km "2)	Forestry Area (K "2)	Corruption control	Government Efficiency	Political stability	Regulatory quality (percentile rank 0-100)
Mauritania	2003	1.82	2801196	1030700	2870	65.5	58.8	43.8	51.2
	2004	2:13	2882186		2770	52.9	48.3	44.7	53.2
	2005	2:40	2963105		2670	53.4	48.3	31.3	49.8
	2006	20:12	3043639		2570	34.5	19	39.9	43.4
	2007	15:14	3120980.983		2470	38.6	26.5	30.8	39.3
	2008	24.76	3200288.305			22.2	14.7	17.7	30
Mauritius	2003	12:59	1222811	2040	374	68.4	73	73.1	71.7
	2004	12.63	1233386		372	64.1	72.5	66.8	65.4
	2005	26.81	1243253		370	66	71.1	66.8	63.9
	2006	51.16	1252987		368	67.5	70.6	65.9	67.3
	2007	115.90	1260692		366	69.6	71.1	71.6	68
	2008	230.07	1268835			72	71.1	75.6	79.2
Morocco	2003	4:31	29520444	446550	43496	53.9	55	39.9	48.3
	2004	9:06	29838668		43568	55.8	53.6	32.7	47.8
	2005	20:59	30142708.8		43640	51.9	48.8	32.2	42.9
	2006	27.01	30,496,553.37		43712	49	54	37.5	50.2
	2007	29.65	30,860,594.59		43784	51.2	51.7	29.3	51
	2008	28.06	31,228,981.41			48.8	51.7	29.2	52.7
Mozambique	2003	2:42	19609837	799,380	193,620	31.1	34.1	48.6	39
	2004	5.60	20078143		193120	27.2	38.9	44.2	38
	2005	14.68	20532675		192,620	32	44.1	48.6	30.2
	2006	14.68	20971449		192120	30.6	41.2	63	33.7
	2007	34.24	21,372,202.42		191620	32.9	41.2	54.8	34.5
	2008	43	21,780,614.04			34.3	42.7	55.5	35.3
Namibia	2003	0.72	1968514	824,290	78098	56.8	62.6	59.1	62.4
	2004	2:21	1993832		77354	56.8	62.1	64.9	58.5
	2005	2:36	2019677		76610	59.2	59.7	64.9	56.1
	2006	6:43	2046555		75866	61.2	61.1	74	55.1
	2007	7:24	2080083.284		75,122	62.3	61.1	81.3	54.4
	2008	19.95	2114160.855			73.4	64.9	80.9	56

Exports diversification index	Foreign direct investment, net inflows (current USD)	Foreign direct investment (% of GDP)	Forestry area (Km^2)	Open a business, (time in years)	GDP per capita (current USD)	GDP growth per capita - % Yearly	Inflation, GDP deflator (annual %)
4.5	214100000.00		396,620		458.80	2.57	2.47
4.2	391600000.00		396,620	8	537.04	2.22	11.54
4.1	814100000.00		397,500	8	619.82	2.57	17.97
4.4	154571179.81		397,420	8	874.80	8.74	29.79
3.9	152876260.42		397,120	8	847.10	-0.63	-2.56
				8	893.08		
13.9	62,630,665.28	1.31	1,060		4291.87	2,13	5.93
11.8	11,164,245.32	-0.30	1,040		4916.83	3.81	5.88
12.3	41,564,676.13	-0.08	1,040	1.7	5059.01	3.74	4.76
12.7	105304322.87	1.51	1,030	1.7	5134.23	2.80	3.81
13.4	338907846.56	4.14	1,010	1.7	5383.15	4.04	7.01
		3.76		1.7	6818.11	4.66	7.61
72.1	2,312,682,906.92	4.62	308,760		1687.73	5.11	0.73
71.6	787050000.00	1.51	300,410	1.8	1908.53	3.68	1.02
63	1,619,750,000.00	2.68	299,890	1.8	1974.73	1.94	1.47
69.6	2,366,000,000.00	3.06	299,460	1.8	2152.28	6.51	1.53
67.3	2,806,640,000.00	2.92	299,600	1.8	2434.13	1.50	3.77
				1.8	2764.40	4.55	3.05
2.8	336698815.00	7.22	488,200		237.95	3.45	5.22
2.6	244700000.00	4.29	489,200	5	283.79	5.37	7.47
3.1	107850000.00	1.64	488,300	5	320.39	5.99	8.78
2.7	153730000.00	2,16	489,300	5	338.32	6.41	9,30
3.5	427360000.00	5.34	488,000	5	374.81	5.02	7.40
		6.03		5	446.97	4.47	6.54
10.2		3.19	388,200		2506.66	2.85	1.01
7.9		3.73	388,200	1.5	3313.12	10.85	1.90
5.9		5.55	388,200	1.5	3595.46	1.22	5.53
5.2		5.06	388,200	1.5	3898.69	5.74	9.17
9.1		8.24	388 050	1.5	4190.84	2.38	9.34
				1.5	4050.72	1.02	11.97

Countries	Year	Chinese FDI	Population	Surface area (Km "2)	Forestry Area (K "2)	Corruption control	Government Efficiency	Political stability	Regulatory quality (percentile rank 0-100)
Niger	2003	12:50	12367244	1267000	12907	12.1	19.9	44.2	23.9
	2004	14:03	12807896		12783	21.8	25.1	27.9	29.8
	2005	20:44	13264190		12659	23.3	24.2	32.7	35.1
	2006	32.99	13736722		12535	16.5	18.5	34.1	26.8
	2007	134.53	14195085.1		12411	18.8	19	24.5	29.1
	2008	136.50	14,668,742.73			20.3	20.9	20.6	32.9
Nigeria	2003	31.98	134659379	923 770	119082	3.4	13.7	5.8	12.7
	2004	75.61	138001086		114986	4.9	13.7	4.3	7.8
	2005	94.11	141356083		110,890	8.3	18	3.4	18
	2006	215.94	144719953		106794	8.3	15.6	2.4	17.6
	2007	630.32	147982941.2		102698	12.1	14.2	4.3	18.4
	2008	795.91	151319499.6			17.9	13.3	3.3	29.5
Rwanda	2003	30.3	8685457	26340	4256	29.6	18.5	14.9	22
	2004	30.3	8819688		4528	37.9	28.4	23.1	28.8
	2005	4.72	8992140		4800	37.4	13.7	28.8	21.5
	2006	7.71	9209997		5072	55.3	43.1	26.4	31.2
	2007	30.7	9454534		5344	58	44.5	38	27.7
	2008	20:18	9720694			59.4	48.3	37.3	33.3
Senegal	2003	2:51	10706962	196720	87,632	45.6	47.9	36.5	46.8
	2004	2:58	10989452		87,182	51.9	51.2	43.3	46.3
	2005	2:35	11281296		86,732	51.5	52.1	41.8	45.9
	2006	4:15	11582863		86282	40.3	48.8	36.1	44.4
	2007	4:39	11893335		85,832	37.7	45	36.1	41.3
	2008	10.61	12211181			38.6	51.2	36.8	44
Seychelles	2003	00:42	82800	460	400	63.1	57.3	63.5	13.9
	2004	00:42	82500		400	61.2	52.6	70.7	23.9
	2005	4:19	82900		400	60.2	57.8	88.5	26.3
	2006	6:46	84600		400	59.2	55.9	84.6	28.8
	2007	6:55	85032		400	58.9	54	82.7	27.2
	2008	6.60	86334.61001			63.8	54	78	27.1

Exports diversification index	Foreign direct investment, net inflows (current USD)	Foreign direct investment (% of GDP)	Forestry area (Km^2)	Open a business, (time in years)	GDP per capita (current USD)	GDP growth per capita - % Yearly	Inflation, GDP deflator (annual %)
2.1	14,912,242.46	0.55	384,120		218.99	0.80	-0.33
3.7	26,330,000.00	0.46	381,120	5	226.19	-4.24	-1.96
2.5	43,980,000.00	1.04	431,170	5	251.05	3.72	6.85
2.5	50,540,000.00	1.41	431,170	5	265.41	2,16	2.58
1.4	27,000,000.00		435,150	5	299.10	-0.04	3,33
				5	365.01	5.96	7.61
1.3	2,005,390,032.50	2.96	739,000		502.42	7.58	11,20
1.2	1,874,030,000.00	2,13	750,000	2	636.56	7.92	20.73
1.3	2,013,370,000.00	1.79	770,000	2	794.08	2.90	19.76
1.2	5,445,340,000.00		780,000	2	1014.85	3.73	19.56
1.3	6,086,730,000.00	3.39	785,000	2	1121.22	4.10	4.81
				2	1401.54	2.96	14,40
2	4655622.79	0.26	18,850		204.54	-1.39	21.86
1.7	7660000.00	0.39	18,800		223.43	3.70	13,14
2.7	8030000.00	0.34	18,800		264.58	5.05	8.90
2.5	11,230,000.00	0.90	18,750		307.76	4.75	9.83
4.1	67,140,000.00	2.35	19,250		360.87	5.15	10,55
					458.49	8.18	17.42
19.6	52,494,809.92	0.73	86,820		640.51	3.93	0.52
19.7	77,030,000.00	0.80	87,370	3	730.70	3.18	0.50
10.4	44,590,000.00	0.60	88,260	3	770.09	2.89	2.27
25.4	220320000.00	2.25	86,380	3	808.66	-0.27	4.29
22.3	78,000,000.00	2.41	86,370	3	950.04	1.93	5.61
				3	1081.67	-0.17	7.33
3.2	58,425,540.73	0.87	60		8523.01	-4.86	5.95
3.8	38,010,000.00	5.70	60		8482.42	-2.50	3.95
4.7	85,880,000.00	7.47	60		10661.26	6.95	17.52
3.2	145820000.00	4.12	60		11439.79	6.12	1.47
3.9	249310000.00	5.68	60		10728.34	6.72	6.68
					9648.69	1.26	25,35

Countries	Year	Chinese FDI	Population	Surface area (Km "2)	Forestry Area (K "2)	Corruption control	Government Efficiency	Political stability	Regulatory quality (percentile rank 0-100)
Sierra Leone	2003		4732526	71740	27931	17.5	3.8	16.3	10.7
	2004	5.74	4925922		2773 8	20.4	10	34.1	15.1
	2005	18:45	5106977		27544	15	8.5	33.2	14.6
	2006	14.89	5270799		27351	11.2	11.8	30.8	14.1
	2007	32.28	5420400		27158	11.6	12.8	33.7	16
	2008	43.70	5559853			12.6	11.4	35.4	20.3
South Africa	2003	44.77	45801325	1219090	92030	64.1	75.8	34.6	67.8
	2004	58.87	46347516		92030	69.4	76.8	40.4	68.8
	2005	112.61	46892428		92030	69.9	75.8	46.6	65.4
	2006	167.62	47391025		92030	69.9	74.9	45.7	67.8
	2007	702.37	47850700		92030	66.7	74.9	46.2	64.1
	2008	3048.62	48687000			65.2	75.4	41.6	71.5
Sudan	2003	00:55	37142156	2505810	687,239	4.9	9	2.4	11.7
	2004	171.61	37899766		681,349	6.3	9.5	4.8	12.2
	2005	351.53	38698472		675,458	3.4	3.8	2.4	9.3
	2006	497.13	39545065		669,568	8.7	11.4	2.9	11.2
	2007	574.85	40432296		663,677	4.8	11.4	2.4	8.7
	2008	528.25	41347723			2.4	5.2	1.9	7.2
Tanzania	2003	7:46	36929648	947 300	360814	20.4	43.1	28.8	37.6
	2004	53.80	37945476		356,692	29.6	41.2	29.3	39
	2005	62.02	39007359		352570	28.6	37.4	33.7	40.5
	2006	111.93	40117243		348,448	42.7	38.9	42.8	41.5
	2007	110.92	41276209		344,326	41.1	38.4	37	41.7
	2008	190.22	42483923			36.2	39.3	45	38.2
Togo	2003	4.73	5698109	56790	4260	27.2	6.2	31.7	21.5
	2004	6:24	5843292		4060	19.4	5.2	31.3	20.5
	2005	4.78	5992080		3860	20.9	3.3	7.2	19.5
	2006	11.72	6144899		3660	12.1	2.4	23.1	17.1
	2007	14:42	6300495		3460	13.5	3.3	27.9	17
	2008	23:12	6458605			15	3.8	39.7	15.5

Exports diversification index	Foreign direct investment, net inflows (current USD)	Foreign direct investment (% of GDP)	Forestry area (Km^2)	Open a business, (time in years)	GDP per capita (current USD)	GDP growth per capita - % Yearly	Inflation, GDP deflator (annual %)
4.5	8615049.67	0.73	28,450		209.43	4.85	8.40
3.4	61,150,000.00	0.80	28,800	2.6	217.84	3.29	15.86
2.8	83,180,000.00	0.60	30,800	2.6	237.87	3.44	12.92
5.3	58,620,000.00	2.25	31,800	2.6	269.91	4,01	11.83
7.3	94,470,000.00	2.41	31,800	2.6	306,90	3.90	10.30
				2.6	351.29	2.43	11.67
54.1	783136092.26	0.14	996 400		3638.62	1.87	4.61
51.5	701420000.00	-0.28	995,780	2	4660.70	3.63	5.55
50	6,522,100,000.00	2.31	995,780	2	5177.84	3.75	5.42
46.7	- 183,630,000.00	-2.37	993 780	2	5438.37	4.21	7.32
45.6	5,745,870,000.00	0.97	993 780	2	5929.77	4.09	8.99
		4.31		2	5684.57	1.29	10.85
1.6	1,349,190,000.00	0.73	1353700		478.71	5.02	9.83
1.5	1,511,070,000.00	0.80	1353370		572.14	3.01	14.66
1.4	2,304,640,000.00	0.60	1368370		707.68	4.13	12.19
1.3	3,534,080,000.00	2.25	1366990		920.51	8.91	6.47
1.2	2,425,590,000.00	2.41	1367730		1143.34	7.75	7.03
					1413.46	5.94	15.76
27.6	308200000.00	3.00	347,210		278.44	2.89	7.14
25.5	330600000.00	2.91	347,500	3	299.15	3.87	8.50
20.4	494050000.00	3.49	347,500	3	362.54	4.45	20,25
31.2	596950000.00	4.17	347,500	3	357.23	3.78	5.28
30.1	646970000.00	3.85	342,000	3	407.63	4.14	8.97
				3	482.31	4.40	8.90
11	33,734,000.00	2.28	36,300		308.69	0.09	-3.25
9.8	57,330,000.00	3.39	36,300	3	352.71	0.44	3.40
13.3	76,990,000.00	4.36	36,300	3	351.83	-1.31	0.92
11.8	77,340,000.00	4.14	36,300	3	360.95	1.32	0.38
9.3	69,000,000.00		36,300	3	396.63	-0.62	1.34
				3	437.13	-1.37	4.41

Countries	Year	Chinese FDI	Population	Surface area (Km "2)	Forestry Area (K "2)	Corruption control	Government Efficiency	Political stability	Regulatory quality (percen-tile rank 0-100)
Tunisia	2003	1:56	9839800	163610	10172	70.9	71.6	51	56.6
	2004	1:28	9932400		10366	65	70.1	53.8	58
	2005	2:15	10029000		10560	57.8	67.3	51.4	51.2
	2006	3.91	10128100		10754	58.7	69.7	58.2	57.6
	2007	3:57	10225400		10948	60.4	68.2	53.8	56.8
	2008	3:57	10326600			57.5	65.4	54.1	55.6
Uganda	2003	1:33	26890404	241040	37,998	25.7	36	8.2	50.2
	2004	00:23	27778909		37134	26.7	37	9.1	52.2
	2005	4.97	28699255		36270	21.8	34.6	10.1	54.1
	2006	14.67	29651734		35406	23.8	37	13	48.8
	2007	18.68	30637544		34542	23.2	39.3	14.9	48.5
	2008	11.98	31656865			23.2	36	18.7	50.2
Zambia	2003	143.70	11218960	752,610	433,416	19.4	19	38.5	28.8
	2004	147.75	11472278		428968	21.4	20.4	43.8	30.2
	2005	160.31	11738432		424,520	26.7	18.5	42.3	25.4
	2006	267.86	12019481		420 072	26.2	25.6	51	28.3
	2007	429.36	12313942		415,624	34.8	29.4	50	29.6
	2008	651.33	12620219			36.7	29.4	54.5	41.1
Zimbabwe	2003	36.74	12510191	390760	181660	5.8	12.3	9.6	0.5
	2004	38.03	12492297		178,530	5.3	10.9	6.7	1.5
	2005	41.63	12475084		175,400	4.9	7.1	6.3	0
	2006	46.15	12459352		172270	3.9	7.6	15.4	2
	2007	59.15	12449219		169140	3.4	6.6	8.7	0.5
	2008	6001	12462879			3.9	2.4	8.6	1.4

Exports diversification index	Foreign direct investment, net inflows (current USD)	Foreign direct investment (% of GDP)	Forestry area (Km^2)	Open a business, (time in years)	GDP per capita (current USD)	GDP growth per capita - % Yearly	Inflation, GDP deflator (annual %)
47.1	540956569.54	2,16	97,840		2539.91	4.94	1.95
44.8	641690000.00	2,11	98,300	1.3	2832.07	5.05	2.60
43.2	785170000.00	2.46	98,240	1.3	2888.41	2.98	3,14
44.3	3,310,610,000.00	10.46	98,270	1.3	3057.06	4.63	3.81
35.8	1,619,610,000.00	4.33	98,260	1.3	3424.80	5.32	2.37
				1.3	3890.94	4.07	5.00
7.3	202192593.62	3.06	124,620		245,70	3.09	7.81
6.7	295420000.00	3.73	126,120	2.2	285.23	3.39	15.35
7.8	379810000.00	4.12	127,120	2.2	321.44	2.92	-1.69
8	393180000.00	6.47	127,120	2.2	335.78	7.23	2.35
10.4	484040000.00	6.16	128,120	2.2	388.16	5.09	7.28
		5.42		2.2	458.95	6.01	6.30
5.8	184000000.00	7.93	254,390		389.86	3.34	19.86
4.1	363440000.00	6.70	254,890	2.7	472.72	3,11	18.73
3.5	356990000.00	4.99	255,390	2.7	609.69	2.81	17.17
2.3	615770000.00	5.77	255,890	2.7	888.17	3.72	13.38
2.5	983860000.00	8.62	255,890	2.7	926.60	3.66	11.80
				2.7	1134.20	3.43	10,75
11.2	3.800.000,00		152,500		591.30	-10.35	377.78
13.6	8,700,000.00		154,300	3.3	377.22	-3.66	381.27
15.7	102800000.00		156,100	3.3	273.99	-5.17	237.95
15.6	40,000,000.00		154,500	3.3			
10.8	68,900,000.00		154,500	3.3			
				3.3			

ANNEX 2

Tables

TABLE A1 - List of countries

Algeria	1	Liberia	25
Angola	2	Libya	26
Benin	3	Madagascar	27
Botswana	4	Malawi	28
Burundi	5	Mali	29
Cameroon	6	Mauritania	30
Cape Verde	7	Mauritius	31
Central Africa	8	Morocco	32
Chad	9	Mozambique	33
Comoros	10	Namibia	34
DR Congo	11	Niger	35
Congo	12	Nigeria	36
Ivory Coast	13	Rwanda	37
Djibouti	14	Senegal	38
Egypt	15	Seychelles	39
Equatorial Guinea	16	Sierra Leone	40
Eritrea	17	South Africa	41
Ethiopia	18	Sudan	42
Gabon	19	Tanzania	43
Gambia	20	Togo	44
Ghana	21	Tunisia	45
Guinea Bissau	22	Uganda	46
Kenya	23	Zambia	47
Lesotho	24	Zimbabwe	48

TABLE A2 - Some Chinese investments in some African countries

COUNTRIES	YEARS	KEY PROJECTS	VALUE (MILLIONS, yuan)	FINANCING
ANGOLA	2004	INFRASTRUCTURE OF TRANSPORT	2000.00	EXIM
	2005	ENERGY	13 000.00	EXIM
	2007	WATER PURIFYING DRINKING	230.00	EXIM
	2008	HOUSES CONSTRUCTION AND RELATED INFRASTRUCTURE	3500.00	
	209	REBUILD ROAD	79.60	
	2009	AGRICULTURAL DEVELOPMENT DURING FOUR YEARS	1200.00	
ZIMBABWE	2001	INFRASTRUCTURE	7.45	EXIM
	2006	AGRICULTURAL EQUIPMENT	25.06	
	2008	OPTICAL FIBER	33,60	EXIM
	2008	MINING	PART OF A PROJECT OF 90 MILLION	CADF
	2009	CREDIT LINE	950.00	
	2009	DONATION	10.00	
CONGO	2000	CEMENT	24.15	EXIM
	2003	DAM	280.00	EXIM
DR CONGO	2000	TELECOMMUNICATIONS	9.66	EXIM
	2007	INFRASTRUCTURE MINING	8500.00	EXIM
	2008	OPTIC CABLE NETWORK	35,00	
	2008	TRANSPORT AND MINING SECTOR	9000.00	

Country	Year	Project	Amount	Lender
	2003	DAM	224.00	EXIM
			PART	
			ON ONE	
	2008	GLASS FACTORY	PROJECT	CADF
			OF 90	
			MILLIONS	
ETHIOPIA	2008	AFRICAN UNION HALL CONSTRUCTION	150.00	
	2008	VEÍCULOSE OFFICE EQUIPMENT		
	2008	INDUSTRIAL PARK	713.00	
	2009	FACTORY	5.20	
	2009	TELECOMMUNICATIONS	15,00	
NIGER	2008	DRILLING RIG AND REFINERY	5000.00	
	2009	DRAFT URANIUM	95.00	
	2001	ELECTRICITY	110.00	EXIM
	2002	ELECTRICITY	150.00	EXIM
SUDAN	2004	DAM	1800.00	EXIM
	2008	EQUIPMENT AND DEMINING TRAINING		
	2008	HOUSES AND HEALTH EQUIPMENT	11,00	
	2006	DAM AND ELECTRICITY STATION	2500.00	EXIM
NIGERIA	2007	COMMUNICATION AND EDUCATION PROGRAM	100.00	EXIM
	2008	ROAD CONSTRUCTION	1000.00	
	2008	POWER PLANT	2400.00	
	2005	DAM AND ELECTRICITY STATION	2300.00	EXIM
MOZAMBIQUE	2006	DAM	300.00	EXIM
	2007	INFRASTRUCTURE	40,00	EXIM

GABON	2008	DAM HYDRO-ELECTRICITY	83.00	
	2003	DAM	600,00	EXIM
	2006	RAILWAY LINE		EXIM
	2007	PLANT INFRASTRUCTURE	206.55	EXIM
	2008	EXPANSION OF POWER STATION	400,00	
ZAMBIA	2008	STADIUM SPORTS	65,00	
	2009	CONSTRUCTION SILOS FOOD	11,60	
	2009	INVESTMENT PROMOTION AND AGREEMENT PROTECTIONISM	3600.00	

(Blanks result from lack of information.)

ANNEX 3

Why the use of the Generalized Method of Moments (GMM)?

The data panel (i countries, t periods) can be described by the following equation (Greene 2002: 307):

$$y_{it} = w_{it}'\beta + \alpha_i + \varepsilon_{it}$$

In this case, represents the set of variables to the right side of the equation, including the dependent variable. It can be proved that for a finite value for T (for example, a short period of time), there is a significant bias on β.

This problem arises when we estimate our data panel by an ordinary regression of fixed effects with a dependent variable. The estimator variance does not move towards zero when i increases. As noted by Greene (2002: 308), this problem is more serious when we estimate our panel through random effects. A common method for dealing with this problem of heteroscedasticity is to differentiate each side of the data panel model.

$$y_{it-1} = \delta(y_{it-1} - y_{it-2}) + (x_{it} - x_{it-1})'\beta + (\varepsilon_{it} - \varepsilon_{it-1})$$

However, it can also be shown that this model has autocorrelation problems between the dependent variable and the deviation of a moving average of the first order.

In addition to the traditional estimator instruments (LSDV or FGLS, discussed in Roodman 2006), other techniques have been developed more recently to produce the GMM estimator (Arellano and Bond, 1991; Arellano and Bover 1995).

With this estimator and a series with a short space, we can use $-y_{it-3}$ or $e^{y_{it-3}}$ as instruments for y_{it-1}.

As Greene (2002: 309-312) demonstrates (reversing formal algebra), the constructed condition of empirical moments, by using these instruments, can generate a GMM estimator that is a robust estimator for panels with reduced temporal dimension. This Annex was largely based on Mourão (2011).

4

Bibliography

- Acemoglu, D., S. Johnson and J.A. Robinson (2001), "The
- Colonial Origin of Comparative Development: An Empirical Investigation." American Economic Review 91(5): 1369-1401.
- Acemoglu, D. (2009), *Introduction to Modern Growth Theory, Princeton: Princeton University Press.*
- Aguiar, Sandra Conraria and Gulamhussen, Mohamed Azzim (2009), *The impact of political risk on Foreign Direct Investment.* Issues Syllabus, Lisbon.
- Arellano, M. and S. Bond (1991), "Some Tests of Specification for Panel Data: Monte Carlo Evidence and an Application to Employment Equations", Review of Economic Studies, Blackwell Publishing, Vol. 58(2), pp. 277-97.
- Arellano, Manuel and O. Bover (1995), "Another look at the instrumental variable estimation of error-components models", Journal of Econometrics, Elsevier, Vol. 68(1), pp. 29-51.
- Alden, Chris, China in Africa (2009), Publisher: Sururu Cultural Productions.
- Bellak, C., Leibrecht, M. & Stehrer, R. (2008), *Policies to*
- *Attract Foreign Direct Investment: an industry-level analysis*, VII Global Forum on International Investment.

- Broadman, Harry G.eIsik, Gozde (2007), *Africa's Silk Road*, The World Bank, Washington.
- Cho Joong-Wan (2003), *Foreign Direct Investment:*
- *Determinants, Trends in flows and promotion policies,* Chap. V Investment Promotion and Enterprise Development Bulletinfor Asia and the Pacific No. 1, Economic and Social Commission for Asia and the Pacific, United Nations, 99-112.
- Davies, Ken (2009), *While global FDI falls, China's outward FDI doubles*, Columbia FDI Perspectives, Available at http: // academ-iccommons.columbia.edu/catalog/ac:125964.
- Greene, William 2002. *Econometric Analysis.* Prentice Hall. NY.
- Hung, Tran Hao (2006) *Attracting FDI in agriculture and rural development- status and solutions for improvement.*
- McQueen, D.J. Grieg-Gran, M. Lima, E. MacGregor, J. Merry, F. Prochnik, V. Scotland, N. Smeraldi, R. and Young, C.E.F (2004) *Exporting without crisis: The Brazilian tropical timber industry and international markets.* Small and Medium Forest EnterprisesSeries No.1. International Institute for Environment and Development, London, UnitedKingdom
- *Main determinants and impacts of Foreign Direct Investment on China's economy,* OECD, Directorate for financial, tax, and enterprise affairs, 2000.
- Mourao, Paulo (2011), "Determinants of the number of Catholic priests to Catholics in Europe - an economic explanation"; *Review of Religious Research*; 52.4; pp.427 - 438.
- Mwilima, Ntawala (2003). *Foreign Direct Investment in Africa*, LabourResourse and Research Institute (LaRRl), Social Observatory Pilot Project.
- Odenthal L. (2001), FDI IN SUB-SAHARAN AFRICA; OECD DEVELOPMENT CENTRE Working Paper No. 173

OECD BENCHMARK*DEFINITION OF FOREIGN DIRECT INVESTMENT*

- Exame Angola Magazine, "The world in 2011". Luanda
- Roodman, David (2006). "How to Do xtabond2", North American Stata Users' Group Meetings 2006 8, Stata Users Group.
- SACHS, Jeffrey D.; LARRAIN, Felipe B. (2000), *Macroeconomics*
- Revised and updatededition. Sao Paulo: MakronBooks.Sebastian, Rajith (2008), "China-Africa Investments - An
- analysis of China's Investment in Africa". ChinaVest
- September 17. Available athttp: //www.amcham- shanghai.org/NR/ rdonlyres/4435B6F6-EB50-46BC- AAF8-0741C1CDBEE1 / 7956 / ChinaAfricaInvestments.pdf.
- vv.aa(2010) World Investment Report. World Bank. Washington.

WEB pages

- About.com:economics
- http://economics.about.com/cs/economicsglossary/g/fdi.
- Economywatch
- http://www.economywatch.com/foreign-direct-invest- ment / definition.html
- The World Bank Group
- http://data.worldbank.org
- Central Intelligence Agency – CIA FACTBOOKhttps://www.cia. gov/library/publications/the-world-fact- book /
- Foreign Direct Investment
- http://www.fdi.net/ ~
- UNCTAD
- http://www.unctad.org/fdistatistics

About the Author

Mauro Santos - Born in Portugal in 1986, raised in Angola, where the author did its first school years, later the author went to study in Portugal International Relations Degree, and concluded a Masters in Public Economics and Policies.

www.ingramcontent.com/pod-product-compliance
Lightning Source LLC
Chambersburg PA
CBHW021457210526
45463CB00002B/810

* 9 7 8 1 6 8 4 7 0 9 9 6 0 *